the Bread Exchange

the Bread Exchange

Tales and Recipes from a
Journey of Baking and Bartering

Malin Elmlid

CHRONICLE BOOKS

SAN FRANCISCO

Library of Congress Cataloging-in-Publication Data:

Elmlid, Malin.

 The bread exchange : tales and recipes from a journey of baking and bartering / Malin Elmlid.

   pages cm

 Includes index.

 ISBN 978-1-4521-1962-5 (alk. paper)

 1. Bread. 2. Cooking, International. 3. Elmlid, Malin--Travel. I. Title.

TX769.E48 2014

641.81'5—dc23

                           2013050332

Designed by Katrin Weber

Front and back cover photos by Mirjam Wählen.

Text on pages 30–31, "Not for Sale" © 2014 by Gisela Williams.

Text on page 81, "Meine Reise zum guten Fleisch" © 2014 by Conrad Fritzsch.

Illustration on pages 14–15 © 2014 by Kheira Linder.

Photographs on pages 2, 22 (top two images), 240 © 2014 by Shantanu Starick.

Photographs on pages 5, 22–23, 28–29, 32–33, 42, 58–59, 60, 64–65, 78 (top right and guestbook), 79 (bunker corner), 92, 118–119, 120–121, 123, 124, 128, 142–143, 158, 160–161, 165, 167, 168–169, 179, 181, 184–185, 191, 195, 196–197, 200, 201, 202–203, 206, 209, 212, 214–215, 226–227 © 2014 by Malin Elmlid.

Photographs on pages 8, 168 (Malin talking with man, Malin with textiles) 182, 206 © 2014 by Matthias Gebauer.

Photographs on pages 13, 216–217, 226 (elevated freeway) © 2014 by Luke Abiol.

Photographs on pages 16–17, 36 © 2014 by Fred Bschaden.

Photograph on page 19 © 2014 by Oliver Helbig.

Photographs on pages 22 (bottom right), 26–27, 34–35, 38, 40, 41, 46, 56–57, 66–67, 70–71, 73, 74, 75, 76, 78–79, 224 © 2014 Mirjam Wählen.

Photograph on page 28 (bottom right) © 2014 by Mary Scherpe.

Photographs on pages 53, 200, 201, 205, 210–211, 220, 221, 228–229 © 2014 by Katrin Weber.

Photographs on pages 82–83, 84, 86, 87, 88, 91, 94–95, 96 © 2014 by Fredrik Skogkvist.

Photographs on pages 98–99, 100, 103, 104–105, 106, 110, 112, 113, 115, 116, 118 (top, couple; toddler standing; bottom center), 119 (horse and bottom center, man in striped shirt), 143 (group, cocktail mixes, bread on board, bottom left) © 2014 by Yorick Carroux.

Photographs on pages 130–131, 134–135, 137, 138, 139, 140, 142 (black and white photo), 145 (hug) © 2014 by Ira Chernova.

Photographs on pages 142 (plated pumpkin salad, women preparing food, portioning ceviche into serving glasses, woman in blue shirt) and 143 (welcome speech, drinks table, bread on table, two women drinking cocktails) © 2014 by Kate Cunningham.

Photographs on pages 146–147, 149, 150-151, 153, 155, 157, 160 (top right, bottom center), 161 (left center) © 2014 by Antje Taiga Jandrig.

Photograph on pages 162–163 © 2014 by Joel van Houdt.

Photographs on pages 167, 168 (truck and people, woman holding bread), 169 (Malin talking with Kabul baker, Malin and others walking in the street, bottom left) 171, 172, 173, 176–177 © 2014 by Farzana Wahidy.

Photograph on pages 188–189 © 2014 by David de Vleeschauwer.

Photograph of Matthias Gebauer on page 230 by Fabian Matzerath.

Photograph of Lotta Lundgren on page 231 by Mikael Grönberg, SR.

Photograph of Mathin Lundgren on page 232 by Salvatore Scappini.

Photograph of Chad Robertson on page 237 © 2014 by Aubre Pick.

Photograph of Karen Boros on page 237 © 2014 by Ralph Mecke.

Manufactured in China   10 9 8 7 6 5 4 3 2 1

FSC® MIX Paper from responsible sources FSC® C008047 www.fsc.org

Chronicle Books LLC

680 Second Street

San Francisco, California 94107

www.chroniclebooks.com

Tell me a story that moves me.
Show me something I have never seen before.
Teach me something I do not know.
Bring whatever you do that you are proud of.

Share with me.
And I will share my bread with you.

I will make you bread out of only water, flour, and salt.
With all my senses I will choose the best ingredients I can find.
I will get up in the middle of the night to fold the dough for your bread.
I will share with you what I do best.

And I will bring a story to inspire you.
Just as you inspire me.

INTRODUCTION

It all started, as many good things do, with a mix of frustration and a lot of dissatisfaction. I was working as a sales manager in the fashion industry, where there is a one-size-only mentality—sample size 4 in North America or 34/36 in Europe. Either you fit in, or you might as well start looking for a new job. Many of my colleagues decided to cut carbohydrates to be able to stay slim and fit in, and so did I. No potatoes. No pasta.

"Is this yogurt unsweetened, sir?" "Oh, no, please no sugar in my coffee!"

I even began to drink my coffee black, as the milk started to seem as forbidden as the sugar. And then bread was off-limits too. That's when it started to get really complicated for me. No bread? I LOVE bread. I grew up in a family where bread is one of the most important parts of our meals together.

For me, bread is the most poetic of foods. It is symbolic of all food, all nourishment. How could I say no to bread? I just could not. So I compromised. I told myself I would only eat *good* bread.

I guess we each have our own opinion of what good bread is, but to me the answer came fairly easily. Good bread is baked with dedication. It is made out of the highest-quality ingredients. It takes time to make and is made with traditional methods. To me, it should be made with wild yeast (known as "sourdough" bread), not because I have anything against eating commercial yeast, but because it is an easy way to ensure that the bread is well made. Baking without commercial yeast demands a good healthy sourdough starter, requires high-quality ingredients, and needs someone with expertise, guts, and feeling to bake it. I promise you can taste the difference.

I don't have to tell you that there is a large variety of good bread available around the world. Bread is somewhat like wine in how we taste it; what we like is, of course, influenced by the other flavors we're tasting. A slab of rye might go better with one style of cheese, such as a strong Gruyère, whereas walnut bread would go perfectly with a runny chèvre. I like all good bread, but I choose my bread depending on what I am eating with it and where I happen to be in the world. During my travels around the world for my work, I fell in love with sourdough bread, made with delicious white flour and risen with wild yeast, simply because it pairs well with a lot of the food I personally like.

This obsession with good bread turned into a little hobby of mine. As I was traveling, it became sport to search out the best possible bread in every city I visited. I made sure to eat my breakfast in the cafés that offered the best bread. I learned that cafés that offer excellent bread tend to have the best of everything else. A restaurant or café that is not investing in good bread is without a doubt cutting corners on quality elsewhere. Bread is the first food a restaurant serves to a customer. Why would any restaurant ever want to spoil the experience by offering anything less than the best in the first bite?

By the time I started my hunt for perfect bread, the trend toward artisan white flour–based bread had already started in many of the world's capitals. In Stockholm and Copenhagen, the sourdough bakeries were booming. In New York City, as well as in London, bread became a topic of conversation. I was able to find good bread when I was traveling to major fashion cities for work, but not when I returned home to Berlin. I was suddenly struck by how difficult it was to find good bread made with white flour in Berlin— or even bread that had been baked with time and dedication. How could this be? In the capital of Germany? A country I consider a "good bread country?"

Don't get me wrong. In Germany, especially in the southern regions, such as Bavaria and Baden-Württemberg, there are a lot of great bakeries that still cherish and use traditional methods. To find a good loaf of dark rye sourdough is fairly easy because the country has a long tradition of baking in that style. However, properly made white sourdough bread was practically impossible to find when I first started looking for it in 2007. Even the best restaurants were serving the saddest looking prebaked-off baguettes. That's why I decided to make my own bread.

So suddenly, I was baking. Well, not *just* baking. I was *maniacally* baking. It was 2008 and my bread baking had turned into a mad pursuit with the lofty goal of achieving the perfect loaf. It was not easy. My trash can was constantly full of loaves that did not make the grade—too flat, too sour, too moist inside, or the crust was boring. They all had to go.

When my loaves did reach the standard I had set for myself, I gave them away. I brought them to friends and shared them with previously unknown neighbors. It went so far that my friends passed them on to their friends because I was simply producing too much bread for our small circle to consume.

And that's how the Bread Exchange started. An acquaintance of one of my friends wanted to return the gift somehow. His father played the viola in the Berlin Philharmonic, so he had two free tickets and he gave one to me. That same week a neighbor of mine came by with a bunch of burned CDs filled with pictures from the German Democratic Republic. He thought that a young foreigner and new Berliner like me, who had never experienced East Germany, might find the images interesting. Maybe that is why the whole project has worked so well. Because the intent was never "to get things." It has been to create a structure for giving others what we have a lot of and for sharing what is important to us. There is something intrinsically unopportunistic about it all. It did not strike me until much later, though, that the Bread Exchange was born from giving without expectation. I think this is the essence and the real beauty of the project.

When I decided to trade my bread, I began by posting about my baking on my blog TheBreadExchange .com. I posted pictures of what had inspired me to make that particular bread and told the story behind every ingredient. My passion for stories and handcrafted quality was immediately fed by all the bread baking. Soon after, I started an online group for the Bread Exchange so I would be able to connect potential traders. We coordinated virtually and met face-to-face to trade. The group became a great way for me to reach people I would never have been able to connect with simply by posting on my blog. I never had an interest in sharing my private life online, but with the Bread Exchange project I learned that the online group was an excellent tool, not only for connecting with other like-minded people around the world but for helping me get more out of my real life.

In my experience, I have found that if you share, you can be sure to get more back one day. Somehow. There is something truly freeing about bartering. The trader has to be creative and think about what he or she is good at and has enough of to share. It is a great pride booster because, as everyone who has made an exchange would tell you, it is a wonderful feeling to trade something you've made or done that is good enough to share.

The Bread Exchange project has introduced me to a large group of open-minded and creative people. It felt natural to produce this book together with the traders I met along the way. Everything I did not photograph or write myself has been traded. This book is therefore just as much a work of the Bread Exchange network, as it is mine.

This book tells a personal story. Every story, place, and recipe in this book was included based on how it has inspired me and the Bread Exchange project. For that reason, the recipe collection is eclectic; together with my recipes, these are the recipes that the contributors wanted to share with me, the recipes that had special value to them. Having now traded more than 1,000 loaves, I have connected with so many inspiring people and places. I could only fit some of their stories into these pages, but even within this sampling and with the handmade bread I will teach you to make, I hope I can pass on some of all the inspiration I have received thanks to the Bread Exchange. The project, and its people, has showed me that celebrating the small, the pure, and the handcrafted that is all around us brings people together, making our daily lives much richer.

I am sure there are places in this book where I could have been more descriptive. I am not a chef, nor am I a professional baker. If you are unsure about procedures, take a minute and search for a more descriptive recipe or how-to video online. Then come back to this book and continue. That is how I work when I cook; I buy inspirational cookbooks and then I find additional help online.

Quality ingredients matter to me and they should matter to you, too. Baking simply demands quality, especially when you are using only three ingredients and no commercial yeast. I use organic ingredients as often as I can. Apart from the obvious good karmic reasons, I think these products are also more fun to buy and generally add more taste. It is never worth it to pick the cheapest oil you find at the market. When I write "pepper" in a recipe, I mean I use freshly ground black pepper, if possible. Invest in a good pepper mill. And don't use fancy salt in the potato-cooking water, as no one will ever taste the difference, but by all means, do use it in your bread. Little touches, like roasting walnuts before you add them to the bread, have a big effect on the final flavor, so embrace these small extra steps. I avoid giving exact measurements for pepper or the butter I use for frying since we all have a different taste for the right amount of these ingredients.

This book is best described as a curated cookbook, a product of the creative contributions of participants and friends of the Bread Exchange. There are as many perspectives on food in this book as there are contributors (so many!). Use them all as your inspiration to try new things and to make things taste the way you like them. Omit what you do not like and add what you think makes it better. Be creative. Make it yours. That is what I do all the time. If you choose a different ingredient or technique than I have chosen, you may get a different result. Maybe yours will be even better.

the Bread Exchange

Bread Exchange Trades

Book Journey of the Sourdough

the Bread Exchange World Map

He handed the tickets to me as we stood in front of the entrance

of the Berlin Philharmonic's concert hall.

They were for two seats in his family's balcony to hear his father,

a famous viola player, play that night.

I followed him through the winding corridors and steep stairways

of the stunning concert building.

We did not know each other.

But I knew that he liked bread. And he knew I loved viola music.

Looking back, I know that night at the Berlin Philharmonic changed my life. One could say it was a coincidence. Before that night, I had no conscious plan to launch the Bread Exchange. I didn't start the Bread Exchange project for any of the obvious DIY reasons, or because of the global economic crisis in 2008; it wasn't inspired by religion and it wasn't a backlash against our consumer society.

The Bread Exchange started because of the huge respect I have for quality and handcraft and the insane amount of dedication that both require. It was simply my own curiosity—and that of those who traded with me—that sparked the beginning of the Bread Exchange. It was born of a decision to walk through life with my eyes truly open, allowing strangers to show me new and unexpected paths.

The Bread Exchange is the most inspiring thing I have ever done. Every trip I have taken has taught me something new. Every person I have met along the way has told me a story that touched me. In addition to flour, water, and salt, I like to think that there is a fourth magical ingredient in my bread: the essence of strangers' tales and unknown places.

Every person I barter with has only good intentions with the trades we make: to share something he or she is really good at, to show me something they think I might like, or to inspire me. What I am given, I use again, either as an ingredient or for inspiration to do something else. The Bread Exchange has become a microecosystem of amazing bread and powerful stories.

Ever since that first trade in Berlin in 2009, the Bread Exchange has spread across the world. I have traded with people on every continent. Of course the exchange could have been about something other than bread. But I think that it is the bread, and the sharing of it, that makes the Bread Exchange so special. Of all the food we eat, bread has the most emotional power. Think about it. How could you *not* share bread? Bread is made for sharing. Believe me, there have been nights when I ate an entire loaf while standing at the kitchen sink with only salted butter as my companion. Those nights were definitely not about sharing, but most of the time a loaf is made for friends and family with the intention of being sliced and shared with everyone around the table. You do not fight someone you share your bread with, or against someone who has shared his bread with you.

The Bread Exchange did grow out of the blog I started in 2008, which I called "miss elmlid, and what to do when it is time off." For me, the blog was a way to hold on to all the inspiring things that were coming my way. I was working long days and traveling excessively for my job, and I had decided that I just could not dedicate myself exclusively to my career. In a world where our identities are strongly connected to what we do for a living, to blog about what I like to do when I wasn't working felt natural. It was simple storytelling, often told through my photography, about the pure things in life that so easily made me forget about time and the pressures of modern work life.

What often matters most to me are the small things. These are the things you can just as easily let pass by, but if you focus on them, or even just notice them, they can make your day.

Most things I choose to do and that I like have a strong connection to quality and history—the fashion brands I have chosen to work for, the houses I have chosen to live in, how I have decorated my living spaces, the places I have decided to visit, and the kind of foods I like to eat. History and quality have been interesting to me for as long as I can remember. As a child I was more keen on spending a Sunday reading the infographics at the historical museum than watching monkeys at the zoo. My fascination with history has developed into a curiosity about the history of items. I believe that disregarding the history of an object, whether it is handcrafted or formed by nature, kills the soul of that object. And when the soul is gone, you can never restore it. Quality and history go together. Everything that has been made with affection has a story to tell. And if something has not been crafted with care and affection, and has no story behind it, it usually doesn't interest me at all! I look for quality in products and the maker's interest in how things are made. I have an enormous respect and love for well-produced things and their details. This is how I like to dress, bake, and even set my table for a meal. Using the butter knife that my grandfather carved out of wood from a cherry tree in his fruit garden, or the wooden basket he made for me to serve my bread out of, gives me so much more joy than using any item I could have purchased. In a world where *everything* can be purchased, these handcrafts are true luxury.

Bread is a food that strongly connects history, storytelling, and craftsmanship. And, more than that, bread emotionally connects a large part of the world, regardless of religion, class, or culture. For all these reasons, I suppose it is not at all surprising that I was drawn to bake and share bread.

In all the trades I've made, there was only one time I felt that the other person had given something without putting thought into his exchange. In *five* years, only *one* person. *That* is impressive. All the other traders have put both effort and devotion into sharing something that is valuable to them. Think about it; the experience of meeting one thousand people who are showing you something special to them, creating something made especially for you. Because of the Bread Exchange, I have had guitar lessons, shared an oven with a star chef in New York City, traveled to places I never thought of going to, and had my bike repaired in a way I could never have done myself. Experiencing such open-heartedness has made it very easy to bake with dedication and to feel deep gratitude for every exchange.

In life, when it can seem hard to let go of control, I highly appreciate the element of surprise in every exchange. Most of the time I have no idea what the barter will bring and I always accept what the barterer wishes to trade. Anything can happen.

POP UP BAKERY

Wild Wood & Bread Exchange
27.3.10

The Bread Exchange was born in Berlin, a city very open to creative ideas of all kinds. It is not a rich city and yet many people are able to live fairly rich lives without earning much money. The creative scene-makers in the city tend to be curious and eager to share without expectations of a reward or commercial gain. Berliners have often traded, either for the lack of money or simply for recognition and appreciation of their creativity. This was a fertile place for the Bread Exchange.

When I began baking, it was primarily to learn how to bake perfect bread. Once I had my method down, I shared the bread I made with friends so that I didn't waste food that I could not eat myself and to get an idea of what perfect bread meant to other people. When I started the Bread Exchange, my intention shifted and I baked to trade the bread.

"Why don't you sell your bread?" is a question I get every other week. Well, you tell me: what would be a fair price for it? I only make two or maybe four loaves at a time. To make one loaf takes me about twenty-four hours. It is true that I do not stand with my hands in the dough the entire time, but to make one loaf of bread I have to schedule my entire day around the process. I often set my alarm so I can wake up and fold the dough at various times throughout the night. I cannot come up with a fair price for a product that requires that amount of time and effort. If I set a price that reflected my investment, and my hourly pay rate, no one would be willing to pay it.

The trades I receive in exchange for my bread are often just as impossible to value monetarily as my loaves. Instead of money, I receive something that is way more valuable to me than any amount of money on this planet. I receive stories, I have inspiring encounters, and my horizons are expanded. I know that if I accepted money for my bread, no one would tell me these stories. I have learned that I value those stories and the inspiration they provide way more than what might be my bread's monetary value. The same goes for many of the people I trade with. With the bread, they receive my story. I have been given honest opinions and ideas. If something is genuinely priceless in our society, it is these honest opinions and the inspiration that the followers of the Bread Exchange have given me. This is what I bake my bread for.

Sometimes the market fails and we do not know how, or are unable, to pay someone a price that is in proportion to his or her efforts, such as the time I spend on making the bread you want or the time you spend knitting a pair of socks that I want. That is when bartering is a great solution. It is often more rewarding for both parties involved.

It might seem unusual that someone with a business degree decided to start a project that accepts anything but money as payment, but when I reflect on this, it all seems totally natural. During my business studies, I majored in marketing and network management. My master's thesis was an analysis on how small creative businesses can build into successful companies by organizing themselves into networks. Looking back, I see the numerous connections between the Bread Exchange and my studies. It is funny how I first came to realize this, years after the project was up and running. I know the Bread Exchange is my hobby, not a business, and there is no monetary transaction but the tools are still the same.

When I look at the Bread Exchange from a theoretical perspective, I love the project even more. It is a perfect example of reciprocal exchange, of well-balanced giving and taking, that network and social exchange theorists might also find interesting. There is no history and no necessary future in the relationship between the people I am trading with.

The Bread Exchange is a loose, anonymous network, where everything is organized spontaneously. There are no contracts or fixed expectations of any sort. There is merely an implicit norm of reciprocity, which is really not a mandate. If you "misbehave" no one will punish you, and no one, apart from me, will know about it. And yet only one person out of one thousand has acted opportunistically. That fascinates me.

It also fascinates me how so many crazy coincidences have happened and continue to happen around the project. A lot of times these happenings seem almost unbelievable. There was the time in New York when I bumped into Daniel Humm from NoMad and, without knowing about his star chef status, arranged to borrow his oven. I believe this shows that if you are open-minded, you will automatically attract and build a network of open-minded people around you. In the case of the Bread Exchange, I think it somehow has to do with the intention of the whole project. If you start with the intention to give and share, you invite richness into your life.

Bartering

Everything Is Not for Sale

by Gisela Williams

When I was a child, bartering was a common practice: trading stickers with friends or Halloween candy with my brother or serving my mother breakfast in bed in lieu of a birthday present. I had no real need for money until I turned ten and then rapidly succumbed to the belief that it was impossible to live without a pair of designer jeans and a branded polo shirt. That was the point when almost everything started to be valued in dollars and cents.

Many years later, when I met Malin in Berlin and was introduced to her Bread Exchange, those memories of trading with friends came flooding back. That initial childish thrill of being able to get something you want without needing grown-up money gradually evolved into something bigger and more complex. I was now forty and raising two young daughters in a foreign city. Exchanging handmade items of value with strangers became something far more valuable than acquiring a coveted object. Somehow when you trade something that you've made with passion for something else that is made with both skill and love, such as Malin's sourdough loaves, much more than goods is exchanged. There is extra value—human connection, conversation, energy, friendship. It's like finding an underground world you never knew existed, populated by a like-minded people. The Bread Exchangers are from all walks of life—they are lawyers, classical musicians, fashion executives, artists, mothers, fathers, and neighbors.

Of course, trading is nothing new. In fact, in many historic communities, grain itself was treated as currency. In the time of the Renaissance, European farmers would bring their wheat to a grain storage, and in exchange they would receive receipts for the amount of grain stored. Those receipts would be used as local currency. That system worked extremely well until the monarchies undercut those community systems by ruling that their own coinage was the only legal medium of exchange.

I've been fortunate enough to travel much of the globe, from Argentina to Indonesia, for my work as a journalist. On these trips I've stumbled upon dozens of fledgling utopian-style projects like the Bread Exchange. We're now at a fascinating crossroads, where many of the world's interesting tastemakers and innovators are looking to the past and using the technology of the present to shape the future. The trend toward artisanal handmade goods started before the global financial crisis but it's only grown rapidly since. The most compelling of these projects are like Malin's: projects in which people make something with great care and love with their own bare hands and then use the Internet and modern technology to create a global like-minded network.

Of course without the help of online networks, Malin would have been unable to touch as many strangers as she has. The Internet is the ideal platform for strangers to trade and share goods and, in some pockets of the world, it has even given birth to gift economies, where goods and services are given without expectations of immediate return.

Although that same technology has slowly worn away at the glue that binds many communities, the Internet has also forged some incredibly inspiring networks on a global level. The truth is that this moment in history is ripe for the concept of bartering to take off. It's clear to many, economists included, that there have to be alternatives to our current fiscal system, which has become so detached from the idea of community and its original purpose: to bind people.

Instead of selling her bread within the traditional economic system, Malin decided to initiate and nurture a bartering circle, which like yeast, has grown and multiplied. She has managed to take these utopian, hippie-style actions mainstream, popping up with her bread in fashion showrooms and five-star hotels. In a world where even the smallest favor seems to have a price, Malin takes a bit of a stand by not putting a price on her bread. A value, yes, but not in traditional currency.

No one is naive enough to think that a Bread Exchange can rebuild a fractured community, but the principles of bartering handmade things in trust with strangers helps create new bonds, whether within small towns or across the globe. It's an idea—exchanging with strangers to create a new kind of community—that is a compelling recipe for bringing more meaning to daily life.

Stockholm Central

the Bread

Good bread is nothing more than flour, water, salt, and dedication. It takes time, but the joy and pride you will get from eating and serving your own bread is incredible.

There are as many approaches to baking sourdough bread as there are sourdough bakers. This is one of the aspects of baking sourdough bread that makes it so appealing to me. There is room for freestyling. Finding the best method for you depends on how you like your bread, and how your life is scheduled. In this book I will give you my personal approach to making basic sourdough bread but, again, this is a subjective perspective. When I started baking, I did a lot of research. I tried so many recipes and methods. In the end, I developed a method that works for me. The basic recipe that I share with you is the one I use everywhere I go in the world. My journeys have been my best teacher. I usually need to adjust the recipe a bit to the conditions around me, but it always works for me. The weather from place to place is always different. The water where I am is sometimes "softer" (has fewer minerals) than the water in Berlin. And the flour I am able to find may have a higher or lower gluten percentage than the flour I am used to baking with. Sometimes I am baking on the road and have to reorder the steps to accommodate my travel schedule. Give this recipe your personal touch. Or use it as it is. You will see how it—and you—can flex in the process.

Bread baking is an art that is hard to describe in exact measurements. Unlike when you bake with commercial yeast, when you work with wild yeast you cannot give precise measurements and times that will work in all conditions. To be able to bake good sourdough bread you simply have to develop a sense for the sourdough's needs and moods. Gaining this sense is one of the beautiful side benefits of sourdough baking. It can be frustrating in the beginning, but you will get the hang of it soon enough.

When you have a handle on how to make the basic sourdough bread, there are endless variations you can make. But how you let your life inspire your bread baking is up to you. Of course your lifestyle will influence the way you bake, too. If you're like me, you are trying to squeeze your baking steps into your daily planning. You will soon see that you can tweak some of the steps in my recipe so that they suit your schedule. You may subtract some hours from the first fermentation step and add them to the last. I do this all the time because my schedule looks different from one day to the next. I also want to use as few dishes as possible (I hate washing dishes!) so I love that bread baking, when done with a kitchen scale, leaves me with nothing but a bowl and my hands to clean up.

There are a lot of good bread books and if you are looking for ones that describe the processes more in detail, I would recommend *Tartine Bread* by Chad Robertson, *Dough* by Richard Bertinet, and *River Cottage Handbook No.3* by Hugh Fearnley-Whittingstall. All three have been a great help for me.

My best advice for getting started is to buy a digital scale so you are able to measure the ingredients in grams. Buy a scale that you can switch between pounds and grams. It will make it easier to use a wide variety of international bread books. When I bake, I weigh all the ingredients since it is the only way to be precise when you measure the flour and salt. I never used a scale before I started baking sourdough bread, but measuring ingredients by weight has been crucial in getting my bread to turn out exactly the way I want it to be. Working this way makes the ratios easier to understand and, later on, you will find it easier to develop your own recipes.

Sourdough

If you are into chemistry and like to keep a lab book, you may want to start a bread baking journal to track your progress. The sourdough trend that took off in Sweden around 2005 started exactly that way—with people like me who wanted to bake bread and began by tracking their developments and results. There was an unlikely stand-out in the beginning: a new father, living somewhere in Stockholm, who had started his sourdough while he was on paternity leave. He had been working in the media industry so the natural step was to start a blog about his achievements at home. Sourdough baking quickly attracted other guys and new blogs followed. Sourdough baking was the trend of the year in 2010. In fact, a similar development had happened in San Francisco in the 1990s when the wild yeast–bread baking trend took hold. It turned out that baking sourdough bread was an ideal hobby for those in the San Francisco Bay Area interested in technology and good food.

Some people say that the baker's relationship with her starter can resemble the relationship to a child. For me that means treat your starter with respect and fulfill its needs. However, same as with kids, do not give it too much attention and don't talk excessively about it with people who don't have a sourdough of their own. There are bakers who have a very personal connection to baking with a sourdough starter. I am often asked if I have a name for my sourdough starter. I do not. Guess I would say that it is manna, after its origin in the Sinai Desert, but calling it by a name? No, I don't! My attraction to baking sourdough bread leans as heavily on science as on emotion. My approach falls somewhere between the analytical scientist or technologist and the big-hearted baker who has a relationship with her starter. I like to understand the steps of baking and how and why they work, but I also have an emotional connection to my sourdough, no doubt because of all the places I have traveled with it in hand.

Why Sourdough?

Commercial yeast was developed to give the baker the ability to command the dough and to take control of the process. A sourdough process demands more of you as a baker. Still, I use only sourdough starter instead of commercial yeast in my bread. Unlike commercial yeast, a sourdough adds a unique texture and flavor, not just air, to your bread. White bread, baked with commercial yeast, is less healthful for you. It is not the commercial yeast in itself that is unhealthful; it is the process of how the yeast saves time that is the issue.

A short fermentation makes the wheat flour in the bread more difficult to digest. Through the long process of sourdough making, the bread achieves a lower glycemic index and the body is able to soak up more nutrition than it does from a bread that uses commercial yeast. The organic acid produced by the lactobacteria in the sourdough helps to activate enzymes, which are already present in the wheat. Sourdough fermentation partly breaks down gluten, making it easier to digest. It is also said to destroy some of the peptides that are believed to be responsible for gluten intolerance. When you consider that your stomach will be able to digest naturally leavened bread more easily, and may not react as it can to pure white flour, you counter the claim that white bread is not good for you.

How to Get Started

You need only minimal equipment to make sourdough bread wherever you are in the world. I always travel with my basic baking tool kit, which I take everywhere with me: salt, linen cloth, wooden board, proofing basket, baking stone, dough scraper, thermometer, scale, large mixing bowl, a lidded jar large enough for 2 to 4 cups/0.5 to 1 L.

The Basic Ingredients

There is a simple rule, applicable to clothes, décor, and practically every simple dish out there: The fewer the ingredients, the more the quality of the ingredients matters.

Buy the best flour you can find. It will be a bit more expensive, but it will make a difference in the way your starter and dough handle and the way the finished bread tastes. I try to buy organic flour wherever I travel and bake. When you're buying flour, always check the ingredients list. The flour I personally want to consume does not contain anything other than milled grain. The microorganisms that are throwing the party in your starter prefer to connect with the shell of the grain, which is retained only in organic whole-kernel flours. Therefore it is easier to get starters going with organic whole-wheat flours.

I try to stick to tap water as long as it is free of chemicals and impurities, rather than spending money on mineral water. However, if you have local spring water in your area that is available in bottled form, I suggest you try it out. The hardness, or softness, of your local tap water can make a difference in your bread, but not so much of a difference that you won't be able to test for the difference and adapt the recipe accordingly. This is what I do all the time when I travel.

I want salt in my bread. But which one? Personally, my purely romantic preference is to use unrefined sea salt. Thanks to all the Bread Exchange traders who brought me salt from around the world, I can say that I have tested my way through the spectrum of fancy salts. I have baked with salt from the Icelandic peninsula Reykjanes, with Himalayan and Peruvian pink salts, and with the most delicate flakes from the Murray River in Australia. I have traded for rough sea salt, collected by the trader and her son on the cliffs in front of their Sardinian summerhouse. I can tell you that you do not taste a huge difference if you did not know where the salt came from, but knowing the salt's provenance does add an extra note to the bread. Still, I can assure you that your bread will be absolutely delicious with standard table salt.

This Is How I Did It

A nice thing with a sourdough starter is that you only need to make it once, because you will reuse the sourdough starter again and again. I have been using (or "hosting," as some say) the same sourdough for eight years. If you take care of your starter, you may never have to make another one. Think about it, your sourdough starter could outlive you. I like this thought. It's like when I was a kid, my brother and I had hermit crabs as pets, mainly because we liked the idea that they might grow older than us. Maybe they would move with us to our retirement home one day. Alas, I have proven to be way better at taking care of a sourdough starter than I ever was at caring for hermit crabs.

A sourdough starter is nothing but flour and water that, by standing on its own for a few days, starts fermenting. You could kick-start the process by adding something sweet, such as honey or pieces of an apple.

When I started to bake, I preferred using my rye-flour sourdough. It was strong, robust, and trustworthy. It always produced a fairly good result: lightly sour, slightly compact, and very tasty loaves. My first sourdough was like a draft horse—sturdy and reliable.

However, that bread soon got a bit boring and I fell into experimenting more with my wheat-flour sourdough starter. This sourdough was fast, sometimes moody, and most of the time very energetic. Some nights it was so active that when I woke up it had taken over the whole kitchen sink. Despite all this, I often got beautiful, elegant, and airy loaves when I baked with it. I would compare its personality to a pure-blood horse. That's who they are, my sourdoughs; the pure-blood Arab and the strong draft-breed Ardennes. I am fully aware that this might sound insane to the uninitiated bread baker.

As you will see in my recipes, I usually bake with a wheat-flour sourdough. In my experience it has been way trickier to make a wheat sourdough starter from scratch than to start one with rye flour. Luckily you can very easily make a wheat-flour sourdough starter from your rye starter, so I will start off by telling you how to make a rye-flour starter and then you can make it into a wheat-flour starter if you like. This is how I started.

Making a Starter

Making a starter begins with making a culture. It's fairly simple: You start the fermentation process with a flour and water mix. As soon as you mix the flour and water, microorganisms that are already present in the flour as well as in the air and on your hands become active. You can use standard all-purpose flour but if you use natural organic flour, without any additives or bleaching, the chance of growing a healthy, natural bacteria culture is higher. If possible, use a whole-grain flour.

Your aim is to develop lactic acid and acetic acid bacteria, which make the sourdough sour and attract wild yeasts that make the dough rise. If you are successful, you will reach a point where the mixture is so sour that no bacteria or mold will be able to grow in it.

Following, I give measurements for how to make your first starter. But personally, I didn't use measurements with my first sourdough starter. I have made my starter in remote locations, such as in the Sinai Desert, where there was no scale or measuring cups to use and still my bread rose and turned out well. However, it can be useful to measure when you are starting out because you will get an idea of how the thickness and overall look of the starter should be at different steps. But in the end, the starter is just flour and water and so my measurements are only meant to be a guide.

Rye Sourdough Starter

Day One through Day Three: Mix ½ cup/120 g lukewarm (105°F/40°C) water with ¼ cup/30 g rye flour. With your bare hands, mix the water and flour together in a wide-mouth glass jar that is large enough for your sourdough to expand to five times the size of its initial volume. Close the lid loosely enough to allow for air exchange. Put the jar someplace a bit warmer than room temperature but not warmer than 85°F/29°C.

Leave the jar undisturbed for about three days. How long you will have to wait to see signs of fermentation depends mainly on the climate. You do not really have to do anything the first day, but it is a good idea to taste and smell the mixture a few times during the second day. If you make a habit of smelling and tasting your sourdough starter, you will very soon understand its different moods, which will be helpful when you bake with it. I know this might not sound very enticing, but learning to understand your sourdough's state will make it easier for you to work together in the future. On the third day, add 1 Tbsp rye flour to the starter and stir.

Day Four: By now you should have some activity going on in the jar. In the morning, stir in ½ cup/60 g rye flour and ½ cup/120 g lukewarm (105°F/40°C) water.

By the evening, the fermentation process should have begun. The best way to test your starter is to taste and smell it. It should taste sharply of acid and smell like a stinky cheese. If it smells like this, throw out almost the entire mixture, leaving about ¼ cup/50 g in the jar. If it doesn't yet smell like sourdough or tastes "off," wait until the next morning, taste and smell it again to be sure it's ready, and then complete the next step: Add ½ cup/60 g rye flour and ½ cup/120 g lukewarm (105°F/40°C) water and mix it all together.

Day Five: By now your sourdough should have grown to nearly fill the jar and should look like a foamy and bubbly mousse. You can now use it for baking (see the recipes for instructions on how much to use), or as a base for making a wheat-flour sourdough starter. If you are not planning to bake when your sourdough starter is ready, then just leave it in the refrigerator until you are ready.

Wheat-Flour Sourdough Starter

Day One: Mix together 1 Tbsp rye sourdough starter, 5 Tbsp/80 g lukewarm (105°F/40°C) water, and ½ cup/80 g organic whole-wheat or unbleached all-purpose flour in a jar that is at least 16 oz/480 ml in size. Once again, don't close the lid completely. Leave the jar to rest in a warm place. Wait until you begin to see some bubbles appear on the surface before you proceed to the next step.

Day Two: Throw out almost half of your starter (yes, you actually discard it) and stir in 5 Tbsp/80 g lukewarm (105°F/40°C) water and ½ cup/80 g organic whole-wheat or unbleached all-purpose flour. Close the lid loosely. Leave the jar to rest in a warm spot overnight.

The next morning, the fermentation process will have begun and your starter will be ready to use to make sourdough bread, or store it in the refrigerator until you are ready to bake.

Troubleshooting

If your sourdough starter is not rising properly but still shows signs of life, indicated by the bubbles in the dough, here are a few ways to rescue it:

» Throw away most of the starter, leaving about ¼ cup/50 g, and repeat the steps from Day Four on.

» Change your flour. Sometimes you are simply unlucky and the flour you bought is old or of low quality. Buy another bag and try again! When I feed my sourdough, I try to use organic whole-grain flour.

» Be patient. When I made my first sourdough starter in Berlin, it took about three weeks until I had a happy and energetic starter to bake with. Sometimes it just doesn't work. Be patient, try again, and it will work.

» If it is cold in your home, try to find a warm spot. When I was in Sinai, I let the sun heat the sourdough as it traveled with me, tied to the saddle of my horse. In my Berlin apartment, I made a cozy corner next to my radiator for my sourdough. A cabinet above your refrigerator might be the warmest spot in your kitchen.

» Don't leave your starter out and then forget to feed it. In order to keep the culture in your starter alive, it is crucial that you feed it and do not leave it out unfed on your kitchen counter if you are not planning to bake with it. If you do leave it out and forget to feed it, throw out about 80 percent of it and stir in 5 Tbsp/80 g lukewarm (105°F/40°C) water and ½ cup/80 g flour. Leave the sourdough starter to rest overnight. Repeat daily until the starter acts like a Day Four starter (tastes slightly acidic and smells fermented).

» Even though you can feed and refrigerate your sourdough indefinitely, you cannot leave it unfed for weeks without risking killing it. If you're unable to bake for weeks at a time, you still need to feed your sourdough once a week, throwing out 80 percent of it and stirring in 5 Tbsp/80 g lukewarm (105°F/40°C) water and ½ cup/80 g flour. Re-refrigerate until ready to feed it or bake with it.

All the white breads in this book are built on one basic sourdough recipe (see page 50). I usually add or subtract ingredients when I bake in different places but I always use the same simple sourdough recipe. If you can master this one recipe, you can experiment with it endlessly. At the end of this chapter, I will also give you a couple of variations on the recipe that I often make and trade in the Bread Exchange. This basic white sourdough bread is my favorite. I prefer to eat it covered in a thick layer of salted butter.

Mixing the Bread Dough

Mix the water, flour, sourdough, and any flavorings according to the recipe in a large bowl. I simply mix everything roughly together with a fork or a spoon. The dough does not really need to be smooth in this step; it just needs to be mixed. You will notice that the dough is sticky at this point. The dough should never feel stiff or crusty; if it does, add a spoonful more water. At the same time it should not be runny. If it is, add a spoonful more flour.

Let the dough rest for at least 30 minutes or a maximum of 1 hour. During this first resting time you give the gluten a chance to develop, reducing or eliminating the need for you to knead the dough. When I first started baking, I think that learning this step kept me from growing impatient with the process. I am not too fond of kneading the dough for long, and I would never bring my mixer with me in the car if I were going somewhere I thought might not have one. On top of that, baking on the road, where sometimes there isn't anywhere to wash my hands, I needed to find alternatives. This "self-kneading" step was perfect.

As a next step, add the salt while folding the dough from the outside in toward the center. Repeat the folding four to six times. The idea is that you fold the dough instead of kneading it. By doing this you will notice that the dough gets more elastic, which enables it to hold its form while baking.

I usually have the dough rest for 30 minutes to 1 hour and then I repeat the folding maneuver again by folding the dough from the outside toward the center four times. Once again, let the dough rest for 30 minutes to 1 hour and then repeat the folding step three to four times during the next 4 hours. Between the rounds of folding, cover the bowl with a lid or plastic wrap so the dough doesn't develop a dry skin on the surface.

After the final folding, cover the dough with plastic wrap or a lid and let it rest a final time. The length of resting time depends on the temperature in the room and the temperature of the water you add. I usually have my dough rise overnight and I try to keep the room temperature no higher than 65°F/18°C. In the summer, as the temperatures go up, it can be difficult to keep the dough from getting too warm when it is left out to rise overnight. Sometimes I set my alarm and check on the dough very early in the morning so I can move it to a cooler spot to finish rising if it is getting too warm.

Shaping

It is difficult to give an exact time when your dough will be ready to be shaped. Assuming that you are using good-quality flour, and that your starter was active, its readiness depends on the temperature. When I had just started baking, I remember finding that instruction unsatisfying. However, it is true. My best advice is to test out the process yourself. You will very soon get a feel for when the dough is ready to be shaped. If the dough is already starting to fall in on itself, or has lost its surface tension and has holes inside, then you know you let it rest too long and the fermentation process has gone too far. In this case, you will need to throw out the dough and start over.

Touch the dough with your fingers. It should not be firm; if it is, it needs more time. If the dough shows tension but retains a small hollow when you gently press your fingers into it, it is ready to transfer to the proofing basket. Place a linen cloth on a flat surface and sprinkle a 50/50 mixture of rice flour and wheat flour on the cloth. Personally, I use either an old linen cloth that I bought at the vintage market and cut into kitchen-cloth size pieces or I simply use a pretty linen cloth my grandmother gave me. Linen works better than cotton because the dough does not stick as easily to it. Now turn out the dough onto the floured cloth. Fold the dough four times, starting from one edge and folding toward the middle. Repeat three times and you should have achieved a nice tension on the surface of the dough (it will be smooth and springy).

Fermentation

I usually leave the dough in the cloth that I used for folding, and place both in a round, linen-lined shallow basket, known as a proofing basket. Of course, you could just as well place the formed dough directly into a well-floured proofing basket. Now your dough should rest again. Cover the proofing basket with a clean cloth. Depending on the temperature, the dough will need to rise 1 to 4 hours, or maybe even longer.

Just as in the earlier step, the proofing time depends on the temperature of your environment. I never check the temperature of the dough, since a large part of the fun of baking sourdough is reading the dough by sight and touch and understanding its behavior. It can seem frustrating to figure out, but when you finally have a handle on the process you can attempt to control the timing by keeping the dough at a temperature that is conducive to your bread-making schedule. If you need to go somewhere, or want warm bread for dinner, you may let the final fermentation take place in the refrigerator, which slows and extends its progress more predictably than at room temperature. I sometimes let the dough rise for 8 to 10 hours in the refrigerator or, if the weather allows it, on the balcony. It is impossible to give an exact time for the rise to be completed; you simply need to develop an understanding of your dough to know its timing. I find my bread often ends up more sour if I let it rise in the refrigerator. I really like this flavor, so I often choose the refrigerator option.

Baking

One way of testing the rise time when you are new to bread baking is to bake one of your loaves a few hours before you think it is fully risen. Later, after more practice, you will have a clear sense of how the dough behaves at each stage and when it is ready to be baked.

I have an old gas oven that is not good for many things, apart from baking bread and giving loaves a really nice dark crust. This proves that you don't need a high-tech kitchen to bake good bread. But if you, like me, want to bake bread with a great crust, you do need an oven that can reach a minimum of 480°F/250°C.

I always bake my bread on a baking stone, which is essential to creating a great crust and interior texture. I even bring a baking stone when I am baking other places than my home. And I have given baking stones to all my friends whose houses I bake at regularly. When you see that your dough has risen and will soon be ready to bake, preheat the oven for at least 40 minutes. My gas oven usually gets hot very quickly, so this tells you how long it takes the stone to fully heat. I place the stone in the middle of the oven on the lowest rack. I put the oldest baking pan I can find directly on the bottom floor of the oven. If you do not have a stone, heat a baking sheet in the oven before you start baking.

Put a piece of parchment paper on a baker's peel, if you have one. (You do not really need a peel; you can just as well use a thin cutting board, flat baking sheet, or something else flat, like the lid of a large shoebox.) Now turn your dough out of the proofing basket onto the parchment paper. I divide my dough in half at this point (since that size loaf suits my household best). Instead of using parchment paper, you may also sprinkle the peel with flour or cornmeal and turn the loaves out of the proofing basket directly onto the peel (and then you will let the dough slip from the peel onto the stone).

If you like, you can now slash your loaves with a sharp knife just before you place them in the oven. Slashing your loaf before baking is a decorative move and a way to put your personal mark on the bread, but it is not essential. I usually do not bother to slash my loaves.

From the baking peel, cutting board, or shoebox lid, slide the dough and parchment paper onto the preheated baking stone or baking sheet. Pour a good splash of water, about ½ cup/120 ml, into the old baking pan on the bottom of the oven. Make sure to do this quickly to keep as much heat in the oven as possible. This replicates professional steam-injecting ovens that introduce moisture as the bread bakes. The water turns into steam in the hot oven, which helps the bread rise and gives it a delicious crust.

Be patient and leave the door closed for at least the first 10 minutes of baking. During this time your bread will rise one last time. After 10 minutes, you may open the oven door but, in doing so, you will let out any steam that is still in your oven. If you like your loaves to have a dark, caramelized crust, leave the oven temperature at 480°F/250°C. (This is what I do.) If you like your finished bread a little lighter in color, lower the oven temperature to 425°F/220°C.

After the first 20 minutes, you may need to turn the loaves front to back once or twice during the remainder of the baking time to enable them to develop an even color. There is no exact time that the bread should be ready. It depends on your oven and on how dark you like your crust. Some baking books suggest measuring the inner temperature of your bread, but I never do this. A good way to test whether your bread is ready is to take it out of the oven and quickly tap on the bottom of the loaf. Because your bread will have lost about 20 percent of its liquid during baking, you'll hear a nice hollow sound when you tap the bottom if it's ready. When I am unsure whether the bread is baked through, I usually bake it a few minutes longer. I'd rather have a darker crust than a doughy interior.

Tasting

There are few things that taste better to me than that first slice of just-baked warm bread spread with a good salted butter. Nevertheless, I think that sourdough loaves taste best when they have cooled down for a couple of hours before they are sliced. In fact, I like to taste sourdough loaves when they are no longer warm to see if they taste even better at room temperature than they tasted when they were still warm from the oven. If a loaf tastes just as good the next day as it did the day it was baked, I know it's good bread.

MY SIMPLE SOURDOUGH BREAD
MAKES 2 LOAVES

This is the basic recipe that most of my loaves are based on. Its simplicity gives you a chance to taste and feel why the ancient baking method is worth preserving. With really good salted butter, it is my favorite meal, too. It is easy to add exciting ingredients to this dough; your favorite olives or walnuts will obviously make a great loaf. However, I believe with the strongest conviction that this bread truly needs nothing added. Not today, not tomorrow, not ever.

½ cup/100 g Wheat-Flour Sourdough Starter (page 45)

1¼ cups/300 g lukewarm (105°F/40°C) water

3 cups plus 3 Tbsp/400 g organic unbleached all-purpose flour

2 tsp/11 g salt

¼ cup/25 g rice flour

¼ cup/30 g any wheat flour

Review the detailed instructions for mixing, folding, rising, shaping, and baking on pages 47 to 49.

Mix the starter, water, and all-purpose flour in a large bowl. Cover with plastic wrap and let the dough rest for 30 minutes to 1 hour.

Sprinkle the salt over the dough and fold the dough four times or until the salt is well distributed and the surface of the dough is starting to feel a bit taut. Let the dough rest for 30 minutes to 1 hour and then fold again. Once again, let the dough rest for 30 minutes to 1 hour, and then fold again and let rest two to three times during the next 2 to 3 hours, covering the dough during each resting period. After the final folding, let the dough rise at room temperature (no warmer than 65°F/18°C) for 4 to 6 hours.

Test the dough to see if it is ready to bake by gently pressing your fingers into the surface to see if it is taut and if your fingers leave a small hollow. If the dough is ready to bake, place a linen cloth on a flat surface. Combine the rice flour and wheat flour in a small bowl and sprinkle the mixture on the cloth. Turn out the dough onto the floured cloth. Fold the dough four times. Repeat three times, for a total of twelve folds.

Transfer the dough on the cloth to the proofing basket and cover with a clean cloth. Let the dough rise at room temperature for 1 to 4 hours, or in the refrigerator for 8 to 10 hours, or longer, as needed.

When the dough has risen and will soon be ready to bake, place a baking stone or baking sheet on the lowest rack in the oven, set an old baking pan on the oven floor, and preheat at 480°F/250°C for 40 minutes.

Put a piece of parchment paper on a baker's peel. Turn the dough out onto the parchment paper and divide the dough into two pieces. If you wish, slash the loaves.

Slide the dough and parchment paper onto the preheated baking stone. Pour about ½ cup/120 ml water into the baking pan on the bottom of the oven. For a dark, caramelized crust, leave the oven temperature at 480°F/250°C. For a crust lighter in color, after the first 10 minutes of baking, lower the oven temperature to 425°F/220°C.

After 20 minutes, check the loaves for even browning and turn them front to back. For even browning, turn the loaves again 10 minutes later. After 40 minutes, remove one loaf and tap the bottom. If you hear a hollow sound, the loaves are ready. If the bread sounds dense, return it to the oven and retest in 5 minutes, and again in 5 minutes, until you hear that hollow sound. Set the loaves on a wire rack to cool. When the loaves are at room temperature, they are ready to be sliced. The loaves will keep, unsliced and stored in a paper bag, at room temperature for 2 to 3 days.

TOASTED WALNUT BREAD
MAKES 2 LOAVES

Of all the nut breads I have baked and eaten, I will probably always love baking walnut bread above all, not only for its taste but also because it is a beautiful dough. The dough gets its dark purple color from the tannins in the walnuts. When you look at the dough after a few hours of fermentation, you will see purple swirls in it.

A really good loaf of walnut bread is made with toasted organic nuts, which can be expensive but are worth it. I love to combine this bread with a nice blue cheese, such as Roquefort. Or why not simply eat it with butter?

Make the dough as directed. When the dough is resting after the first folding and you have added the salt, toast the walnuts in the oven in a baking pan or on top of the stove in a large sauté pan or skillet. (Of course, you can just as well prepare the walnuts in advance if you prefer.) To toast in your oven, preheat the oven to 400°F/200°C. Spread the nuts in the baking pan and stir them every 4 to 5 minutes so they do not burn, removing them when they smell fragrant and the meats are golden brown. To toast on the stovetop, heat a sauté pan or skillet over medium heat and add the nuts, stirring frequently until well toasted. Let cool. You can now decide to cut the walnuts in rough pieces, or as I do, to break them in half, or to keep them whole.

During the last fold, add the walnuts, poking any pieces into the dough that are not folding in naturally. Complete the recipe and bake as directed. Set the loaves on a wire rack to cool. When the loaves are at room temperature, they are ready to be sliced. The loaves will keep, unsliced and stored in a paper bag, at room temperature for 2 to 3 days.

1 recipe My Simple Sourdough Bread dough (see facing page)

1½ cups/150 g walnuts

THE BREAD EXCHANGE SOURDOUGH BREAD
MAKES 2 LOAVES

The first time I baked this bread was in Paris when I shared a showroom with the United Kingdom apparel label Peter Jensen. My friend Gerard Wilson, who works with Peter, shares my dedication to bread baking, and that year we had decided to skip the usual catering company and instead serve our clients homemade bread.

One evening, I got the idea to color my dough with an edible charcoal powder I had received as a trade from a Bread Exchange follower in South Korea. My mother always does this trick with saffron, simply to extract the color; it enables the powder to blend better with the water in the dough. I use a splash of rum or vodka, but you can use whatever you have on hand. If you do not want to use alcohol, you can just mix the charcoal with water; it may not dissolve perfectly, but the result will be beautiful, too. In the morning, the dough had developed an elegant gray tone, which I knew would perfectly match not only the marillen marmalade I had received in trade from a French client the day before, but also Peter Jensen's spring collection. As Gerard entered the kitchen and saw my gray dough resting in the bowl, he clapped his hands and exclaimed in a tone that only an Englishman can manage, "Oh, Malin, what a perfect Dior-shaded dough!"

This bread, with its crust covered in sage leaves for decoration, has become the signature bread for the Bread Exchange. This is the bread I bake the most and it is often requested as trades. Just as for a white sourdough loaf, you can serve it with practically anything. It is the most beautiful background color for a slice of salmon, a beet mousse, or practically any jam. I like that the charcoal powder does not substantially change the taste of the simple sourdough. Some traders say they taste no difference, some say they do.

I think that the charcoal lessens the sourness of the bread a tiny bit. However, the blind tests I've done with traders seem to show that the black color only makes us imagine a difference in the bread's flavor. You can find edible charcoal powder at natural foods stores and online.

1 tsp edible charcoal powder

2 tsp any alcohol in your bar, such as rum or vodka, or water

1 recipe My Simple Sourdough Bread dough (see page 50)

Large leaves from 2 sage stems

In a small bowl, mix the charcoal and alcohol together.

Prepare and bake the dough as directed, mixing the charcoal-alcohol mixture in with the water and arranging the sage leaves over the tops of the loaves. Bake as directed.

ROSEMARY BREAD WITH GOJI BERRIES
MAKES 2 LOAVES

As much as I hated rosemary as a child, I love it today. Rosemary bread was one of the first breads I baked. People know this about me, so I often receive rosemary plants in trade. So far I have managed to use them all. I like to keep the rosemary in this bread very roughly chopped, and a lot of times I do not chop it at all; I just rip the leaves from the sprigs and add them in whole.

In 2010, I traded my bread for a goji berry tree from an organic goji berry nursery close to Hamburg, Germany. I had always thought these berries only grew in Asia, but I have since learned that you can them find growing wild in the parks in Berlin. (Though you may be able to find them growing wild in your area too, make sure to use organic goji berries to be certain that they are not full of pesticides.)

In the beginning, I mainly used the gojis for smoothies or muesli (see page 111), but I soon started to experiment with them in baking. I developed this version to introduce even more moisture into the bread, as the soaked goji berries hold a lot of water. Together with the rosemary they make for a beautiful, fragrant loaf with a warm red color. I serve it with everything from smoked ham to mature goat cheeses, such as Pouligny Saint-Pierre.

⅔ cup/70 g dried goji berries

1 recipe My Simple Sourdough Bread dough (see page 50)

1½ Tbsp coarsely chopped fresh rosemary

Soak the goji berries in water to cover them them in a glass that is large enough for them to plump and enlarge.

Start making the dough as directed, but reduce the water to 1 cup plus 2 Tbsp/250 ml.

After the first folding of the dough, the goji berries should have softened. Drain the berries, reserving the soaking water for another use. (I usually add the soaking water to smoothies because gojis contain healthful antioxidants and the soaking liquid adds a nice earthy taste.) During the second series of folding, add the gojis and the fresh rosemary to the dough. Don't worry if the dough feels as if it will fall apart from the new liquid; it will tighten up during the folding and the fermentation process.

Complete the recipe and bake as directed. Set the loaves on a wire rack to cool. When the loaves are at room temperature, they are ready to be sliced. The loaves will keep, unsliced and stored in a paper bag, at room temperature for 2 to 3 days.

FINNISH COMFORT BREAD
MAKES 2 LOAVES

When I was a child, my favorite bread was the kind that my father brought back from business trips to Helsinki. It was a fairly dark, dense, flat sourdough bread very unlike the kind of sweet and fluffy bread commonly available in Sweden at that time.

I remember making a whole tray of slices with cream cheese and fresh sprouts for my brother and me to enjoy. It was our comfort food. That dark, dense bread is still one of my favorite breads. I never traded it with the Bread Exchange network, but was once brought a loaf from a follower from Finland. In fact, it is the only bread that anyone has ever offered in trade (so far!).

To make the predough: In a large bowl, mix the sourdough starter, water, and rye flour into a thick dough. Cover the dough and let it rise at room temperature for at least 12 hours, or up to 2 days. In my home, it usually rises for approximately 14 hours. It will become much looser, bubbly, and acidic-smelling after 12 hours. You can now decide to bake with it or let it rest even longer, depending on how intensely sour you want the bread to taste.

In a medium bowl, mix the water and sourdough starter. Gradually add this mixture to the predough and mix well. Add the rye flour, a little at a time. Transfer the mixture to the bowl of a tabletop mixer and knead, or knead by hand, for 10 minutes. Add the salt and knead for another 5 minutes. Let the dough rest for 1 hour.

Turn the dough out onto a well-floured work surface. Divide it into two pieces and, using a dough scraper, fold each dough piece over on itself a couple of times. (The dough is fairly sticky at this point, so if I am on the road and don't have a good work surface, I skip this shaping step and just use my wet hands to lift the dough out of the bowl and onto pieces of parchment paper.) Sift plenty of rye flour over the dough.

Cover with a kitchen towel and let rise until doubled in size, 1 to 1½ hours at room temperature or overnight in the refrigerator (which increases the sourness). Personally, I like my comfort bread sour, so I refrigerate the dough overnight.

Place a baking stone or baking sheet in the oven, set an old baking pan on the oven floor, and preheat the oven to 480°F/250°C. Slide the dough off the parchment paper and onto the preheated baking stone. Pour about ½ cup/120 ml water into the baking pan on the bottom of the oven. Immediately lower the temperature to 400°F/200°C. Bake the loaves for about 1 hour, or until they sound hollow when tapped on the bottom. For a darker crust, bake the bread for about 1 hour 10 minutes. Set the loaves on a wire rack to cool. When the loaves are at room temperature, they are ready to be sliced. The loaves will keep, unsliced and stored in a paper bag, at room temperature for 2 to 3 days.

PREDOUGH

½ cup/100 g Rye Sourdough Starter (page 44)

½ cup/120 g water

1⅓ cups/160 g whole rye flour

1 cup/240 g water

¼ cup/50 g Rye Sourdough Starter (page 44)

2⅓ cups/290 g fine rye flour, plus more to sift over the dough

2 tsp/11 g sea salt

the Sinai

The Beginning of It All in the Sinai Desert, Egypt

The Sinai Desert is full of stars.

And it is full of captivating stories.

Some tell us about our collective heritage, such as how the first bread in history was baked here thousands of years ago.

Many of the stories are religious, such as the one about how Moses led his people from Egypt to Israel and how they survived the hunger, thanks to manna, the bread from Heaven.

And then there is also my story—

the story of how I started a sourdough in a jar, tied to the back of my horse's saddle.

As so often occurs, vital things seem to happen when we least expect them to. I had left Berlin to get some time off after a heavy work period. I wanted to exercise, get a dose of excitement, and be on my own. So I decided to go on a horseback-riding trip in the Sinai Desert.

I had already been traveling with my sourdough starter around the world for several years, so I thought it was about time to take a real holiday—one away from my sourdough. I had promised myself I was not going to bake this time. No alarms waking me up to fold the dough in the middle of the night. No broken sourdough-jars ruining my suitcase and clothes. The sourdough was left at home in the refrigerator in Berlin. This is what I imagine holidays without kids are like for parents: Freedom.

The trip to Egypt was exactly what I needed. I woke in the cold morning, around four o'clock, and took off on my horse to watch the sunrise from a cliff an hour away. My horse and I rested during the hottest hours so we would have enough energy to ride back in the afternoon. I felt like I could never get tired of the feeling.

I do not know what got me itching to bake again. Maybe it was that dawn when I was riding through the desert. The air was cold but the horse's back was warm and I kept myself wrapped in a light wool blanket. The sky was dark and so clear that it felt like I could count every star I saw. I could not help thinking about how this was the birthplace of bread. I do not know why, but I get completely drawn in when I feel a connection to the past, whether it's actual history or just someone's beautiful stories.

Overlooking the never-ending path in front of me, I also could not stop thinking about being in the land of manna. This was where the Israelites traveled to get from Egypt to the land of Canaan, guided by Moses. The book of Exodus in the Bible tells how they almost starved to death in the wilderness of Sinai—until, that is, Moses turned to God and asked for help. More than 2,000 years ago, right here, on the same sand as I was riding on, the people of Moses had been gathering an edible fresh frost that covered the ground. The Israelites called it manna, the bread from Heaven. For forty years in the desert, the manna saved them from starving, and it was to be collected every morning before it melted away in the sun. In fact, not only the Bible mentions this; the Quran also tells us how manna was sent by Allah, through Moses, to the people of Israel. As with most things, there is probably a logical explanation for what seems to be a wonder, and scientists of today have a list of fairly probable explanations for what that manna could have been.

As the daughter of two natural scientists, I know that believing in science does not necessarily make me the most creative person. And believing purely in science is definitely less fun. So in the darkness, on my horse, I elected to believe that manna was the bread sent by a higher power. And I decided to test my theory.

The next morning I did not get back on the horse. Instead I decided to break my promise not to bake for two weeks and headed off to try to make a sourdough starter from scratch in Sinai. For anyone who isn't a committed bread baker, this might look like an addiction. Some sourdough bakers would call this a classic cold-turkey reaction. Maybe I was too weak to resist. I like to think I just realized the specialness of the situation and seized it.

To make a sourdough starter, I needed three ingredients: flour, water, and a suitable fruit. Fruit is not really necessary, but it is an easy way to kick-start the sourdough fermentation. I asked the mama of the house where I was staying if she had an old glass jar for me to use. I then went out to search for ingredients. Finding the fruit was not too difficult; I bought an apple (imported from Syria). Finding suitable flour was, however, quite a task. At home, I was mainly used to sourdoughs based on wheat or rye flour, and rule Number One for selecting flour was that there should be no additives. Rule Number Two was, if possible, that the flour should be organic. But here, in Sinai, I had to take what I found.

I cut one-third of the apple into very fine pieces and mixed it with the flour and the water. I placed the jar next to my madras and went to sleep. From then on it all went so fast that it almost felt like magic. When I woke up the next morning there were already small bubbles on the inside wall of the glass jar. I could not believe it! I smelled the sourdough but at this point there was not much more smell than a hint of olives, which must have been stored in the jar before it was given to me. It still needed some time but I knew I was on the right track. I threw out about half of the starter and added a couple of tablespoons of new flour and the same amount of water. Since I did not have a scale I had to improvise.

When I looked at the jar that evening, my sourdough was bubbling and foaming like an airy chocolate mousse. It made funny, burbling sounds. It was ready to be baked with. I was filled with respect and humility for the natural process. What normally takes about a week at home in Berlin had taken just twenty-four hours in the Sinai Desert. With all the stories of manna in my head, at that point I could do nothing but choose to believe in them.

The last days of my horseback-riding holiday in Egypt turned into a never-ending baking session. I was glad to be traveling on my own, so no one else was subjected to my mania. I made a dough from my starter and went out to search for a baker who would let me use his wood-fired stone oven. I found a restaurant I thought was small enough to be open-minded to my madness. With the dough hidden under a scarf, I edged into the kitchen to see if I could convince the young man in charge to let me use the oven. He was surprisingly quick to let me use his tools and followed my moves curiously. The oven was burning hot and I had never before baked over an open fire. The loaf turned out far from perfect but it was real bread. And I was so proud of it. I shared the loaf with my host, the sweet English lady who was also on the trip, and the horses.

So, what happened to that sourdough starter I made in Sinai? Well, after my experience in the desert, I felt almost spiritual and had to honor the feeling. I divided my starter into thirds and left one part behind in the desert. One part I left with the lovely English lady (who was traveling on her own after having lost her beloved husband earlier that year). The third portion I brought home with me to Berlin.

And this sourdough starter, which I call Manna, is the mother of every loaf I have baked and traded ever since.

CHEESE PHYLLO SQUARES

Contributed by Nicole Salazar and Teta Samira, **MAKES 28 SQUARES**

I met Nicole in Berlin when she traded Patti Smith's book Just Kids *with me for a loaf of sourdough bread. Nicole carried the loaf with her back to the States and shared it with her relatives.*

When I was throwing a potluck afternoon in New York City half a year later, Nicole brought an Egyptian dish that her grandmother, who lived in the Garden District in Cairo, used to make for their Peruvian-Egyptian family feasts back in NYC.

Preheat the oven to 350°F/180°C.

In a food processor, pulse 4 oz/115 g of the gibna until smooth. Add the cream cheese, ricotta, and mint and continue pulsing until well-blended and clump-free. Taste the filling and add in the remaining gibna, piece by piece, pulsing until smooth after each addition, and tasting each time until the desired saltiness is reached.

Carefully lay a phyllo sheet on an ungreased 13-by-18-in/33-by-43-cm baking sheet. Brush clarified butter onto the phyllo sheet, starting at the corners and brushing toward the center, then along the edges, and finishing with lightly coating the center. Working quickly, place another phyllo sheet on top, smoothing gently. Repeat brushing the butter, layering a total of ten phyllo sheets. Keep the unused phyllo covered with a damp towel to prevent it from drying out.

Spoon the cheese filling on the top phyllo sheet, spreading evenly and leaving about ½ in/12 mm between the filling and the phyllo's edges. Sprinkle the Parmesan over the filling.

Gently lay a phyllo sheet on top of the filling and repeat the brushing process, laying down the remaining nine sheets.

Fully brush the top phyllo sheet and let rest, uncovered, in the refrigerator for 10 minutes. The top layer of clarified butter should congeal before you continue.

Cut the phyllo into 28 small squares, approximately 3 by 3 in/7.5 by 7.5 cm. In a small bowl, whisk together the egg and milk. Pour the egg mixture over the phyllo, distributing it evenly over the squares. Run the knife along the cuts once more, allowing the egg wash to seep through.

Bake 40 to 50 minutes, or until the top is golden brown and the bottom is fully cooked through. Serve warm.

8 oz/230 g gibna domiaty, or other creamy feta cheese, crumbled

8 oz/230 g cream cheese

12 oz/345 g ricotta cheese

1 Tbsp crushed, dried mint

Twenty 12-by-17-in/30-by-43-cm sheets phyllo dough, thawed if frozen

8 oz/220 g melted clarified butter, plus more as needed

2 Tbsp grated Parmesan cheese

1 egg

½ cup/120 ml milk, at room temperature

>> If making ahead, wrap the tray tightly with plastic wrap after it has rested in the refrigerator. The squares can be made up to this point as early as 3 days before you plan to bake and serve them.

>> When preparing the filling, a fork and bowl can be used instead of a food processor, although it will take more care and a bit more time to ensure the filling is well blended. If you are blending by hand, let the cheeses come to room temperature to aid the process.

Berlin

Bread Exchange Dinner in Berlin, Germany

I moved to Berlin on October 3, 2000, the tenth anniversary of the reunification of Germany. I had just turned twenty and wanted to take a year off before going to university. It was a good day to arrive. The city was celebrating and the parade avenue Unter den Linden was turned into a car-free zone to honor the occasion. The sun was shining and the sky was a crisp blue.

On that first day's stroll through the former East Berlin, I walked by a bombastic concrete colossus just around the corner from my own flat. It was four stories high. I guessed it was a bunker from World War II, standing on its own in the middle of a central resident zone. It made an impression on me from that first moment and I wanted to know its story.

I wish the buildings in Berlin could tell their stories. So much has happened here. The buildings are so much more than concrete, architecture, and stone. Like the people of the city, they too have had to adapt to the ever-changing political colors, adjusting their purpose along the way. It has happened again and again.

It was Berlin's complex history that compelled me to move here in the first place. The National Socialism era and the World War II and post-war history is present throughout the city. Berlin has been a city of constant change. The German capital is today known for its creative scenes and opportunities. But from a historic perspective, this is nothing new. Before the World Wars and the Wall, Berlin was an international cultural center on many levels. You can feel this. And you see it in the architecture.

The rent for my first flat in Berlin was cheaper than the rent for a small student dorm room in Sweden, and was located on Rosenthaler Strasse, in the middle of the former East Berlin. The three-room apartment had old wooden floors and a 13-ft-/4-m-high ceiling. It was something I couldn't dream of affording in London, New York, or Stockholm. The walls, with their unrepaired bullet holes, were left completely rough. Every morning I woke up with chalky bits from the crumbling concrete walls in my bed. The apartment was heated with coal, which had to be carried up from the basement; something I chose to see as part of the charm of the place. It was hard work, but my roommate and I made it fun. We threw weekly dinner parties that began with everyone carrying up heavy loads of coal. I remember how my parents shook their heads when they visited me for the first time. But I was so in love with the city that I never wanted to leave.

The bunker I saw on my first day in Berlin was one of those buildings with stories to tell. Built by mandatory labor in 1942, it served as a bomb shelter during World War II and was later turned into a prisoner-of-war camp, controlled by the Red Army. Later, during the GDR's control of East Berlin, the bunker was used to store dried "exotic" fruit. Maybe this was one of the highlights for the bunker, when you consider how difficult it was to get any fruit, especially bananas, in the GDR. When the wall came down, the bunker was once again taken over, but this time it was turned into an illegal techno club. The party continued until the police ended the fun in a raid in 1996, forcing the club to close.

Shortly after my move to Berlin, art collectors Karen and Christian Boros bought the bunker and converted it into an exhibition space for their private collection of contemporary art. The 32,000 sq ft/3,000 m² of modern art turned the bunker into a statement of what Berlin is today: a city full of creativity and contrasts. This kind of reinvention was happening all over the city, and it was the ideal environment for starting the Bread Exchange.

I could have started the Bread Exchange anywhere on the planet, but Berlin played a major role in the swift growth of the project. Somehow, even with all the prevailing limitations of this German city, creativity is always supported. Berlin has a climate that nourishes new ideas. The reasons are easy to pin down. Unlike many other capitals, the city is affordable, which enables creatives to work at their own pace. There are fairly low rents and a lot of empty space to use for any spontaneous project. In a city that lacks funding—Mayor Klaus Wowereit calls it "poor but sexy"—trading is nothing new. In Berlin, products, ideas, and handwork are often bartered out of need.

Obviously this behavior is not exclusive to Berlin. Nor is it new. Shortly after World War II, in 1948, the black market in Berlin accounted for one-third of the city's economy. In fact, the German economy would rely on the black market for another decade. Along the railway by Alexanderplatz, by Tiergarten, and at the Brandenburg Gate, everything was offered for sale or barter, including foodstuffs such as butter, meat, and vegetables and luxury items like margarine, sugar, and women's stockings. Cigarettes were forbidden, so a pack of Chesterfields would go for up to 200 Reichsmark (the equivalent of $60).

Today, flea markets have become ingrained in Berlin life. Like traders, these vendors seem to represent the spirit of makeshift DIY culture in Berlin. When you can't find everything you are looking for, you simply have to make it yourself. And make the best out of what you have. Before a building slowly falls into ruin, you turn it into a techno club. When wild-yeast white sourdough bread is hard to find, you make your own. Berlin is a hands-on city. I love this, Berlin's unpredictability and mutability. And Berlin's curiosity. There is no fear of the new. One thousand strangers have eaten the bread of the Berlin-born Bread Exchange. They have met me early in the morning and late at night at cafés, in subway stations, and at my home, among many other places. And all out of curiosity, trust, and interest in finding what they cannot find anywhere else in our city.

GOJI-INFUSED RUM SHRUB

Contributed by John Benjamin Savary, **SERVES 15 TO 20**

It was Benny who gave me the idea to bake with the goji berries in 2010 when he invited me to join him to visit a goji berry field somewhere between Hamburg and Berlin. I brought goji berry bread to give to the farmer, who ended up making us honorary godparents to his small organic operation. When I asked Benny to make a cocktail out of goji berries, he was easy to convince.

The result of Benny's experimentations, a goji-infused rum shrub, is a light, fruity cocktail with umami undertones that come from bracing vinegar and the berries' intriguing, cereal-like notes. Although you make the shrub 12 hours before you serve the drink, the rest of the preparation is lightning-quick, making it a perfect dinner party aperitif or a great sunny afternoon poolside companion.

Sure, it's a bit of a shock to throw the shooting star of the superfood family into a boozy cocktail. Drowning these tiny antioxidant bombs in alcohol is a bit like forcing a monk to watch a Black Sabbath gig, but the combination works despite the unlikely pairing.

4 cups/910 g fresh strawberries, hulled and quartered

1 cup/100 g dried goji berries

4½ cups/1 L bottled water

4½ cups/1 L Bacardi Superior Rum

5 cups/1 kg granulated sugar

2½ cups/600 ml distilled white vinegar

Ice cubes

3 to 4 bottles dry Prosecco (or up the posh factor with Champagne)

Lemon balm for garnishing

Pour the strawberries (reserving eight to ten for garnishing), goji berries, water, rum, sugar, and vinegar into a large container. Stir until the sugar has completely dissolved. Cover and leave to infuse in the refrigerator for at least 12 hours. Taste and stir every 2 to 3 hours, if you like!

When you're ready to dole out the drinks, completely fill large tumblers with ice cubes. Fill the tumblers halfway with the prepared rum shrub. Top off with the Prosecco, give each drink a quick stir, and then add a couple of reserved strawberry quarters and a sprig of lemon balm. That's it!

≫ You may tweak the rum shrub–to–Prosecco proportions to taste. More bubbly will add a more pronounced acidic kick to the drink.

≫ For the vinegar, any basic supermarket brand with 4 to 5 percent acidity will work.

≫ While rum shrubs are just as tasty when prepared with nothing but strawberries or their wild equivalent, goji berries add a wonderful note and twist to the finished bouquet.

≫ If fresh strawberries prove hard to find, frozen ones work equally well. Freezing perforates their cell membranes and ensures that the berries release their aroma even more quickly than fresh fruit.

≫ Leisurely souls keep their rum shrub in the refrigerator for up to 2 days, but please remember to remove all fruit after 24 hours so it doesn't totally deteriorate. And don't soak fruit that will be used for decoration, because soaked fruit loses color and crispness.

Fig Confit
by Anna

FIG CONFIT

Contributed by Anna Küfner, **MAKES 2 CUPS/570 G**

Anna called me up in 2011 because she was catering the opening of a Berlin art gallery and wanted to trade bread for it. Her idea was to make a bread installation to show different taste combinations of bread and cheeses. She had heard about my bread but had never tried it herself. We thought it would be interesting to see how the guests would react when they could select from fancy bread with delicate cheeses.

Instead of pairing my most simple white sourdough bread with cheese, Anna chose to serve it with salted French raw-milk butter. The bread-and-butter combination was gone in seconds, long before the excellent selection of French raw-milk cheeses.

There are moments, and breads, that are simply made for specific cheeses. If, like me, you sometimes crave goat cheese so mature that you think it might walk out the door the minute you turn your back on it, then this Fig Confit is the ideal accompaniment.

Combine the fresh figs, pears, and apple in a medium stockpot and stir in the sugar. Leave the mixture to steep for at least 1 hour, until the fruit becomes juicy and the sugar has dissolved.

While the fruit is steeping, in a small bowl combine the ground mustard seeds with the vinegar to release the essential mustard oils.

In a blender, purée the dried figs and apple juice until smooth.

Add the blended figs and the vinegar mixture to the stockpot and heat it slowly over medium-low heat. When the mixture begins to boil, lower the heat and let it simmer for 45 minutes, stirring from time to time. Mash the mixture gently with a hand masher, add the thyme leaves and lavender honey, and let it simmer for 10 to 15 minutes. The texture of the finished confit should be soft but not liquid. Season the confit with some fleur de sel at the end of the cooking process. Let the mixture cool, and then spoon it into clean preserving jars and store in the refrigerator for up to 1 week.

3 fresh figs, stemmed and diced

2 ripe pears, peeled, cored, and diced

1 apple, peeled, cored, and diced

½ cup/100 g raw cane sugar

6 Tbsp/50 g mustard seeds, ground

Splash of white wine vinegar

2 dried figs, chopped

Splash of apple juice

Fresh thyme leaves from 2 sprigs

1 Tbsp lavender honey

Fleur de sel

>> The confit goes excellently with aromatic blue cheeses as well as with mature goat cheeses.

DAAL WITH VEGETABLES
Contributed by Karen Boros, **SERVES 8**

When contemporary art collectors Karen and Christian Boros threw the opening party for the second exhibition of their collection in 2012, and Karen called to ask if I could bake the bread for the opening, I asked how many people were invited. "Three hundred fifty," she replied. I took a deep breath. How would I, in my normal home kitchen, be able to bake bread for so many people? The German art and media scene was invited, and I was curious to see if they would like my bread, so I was torn. "I do not think I can manage to bake more than thirty loaves in one day," I explained, but my mind raced as I imagined how I could manage the challenge.

"How could I pay you?" Karen asked me. "I do not take money, but I am sure there is something that we can find as a good trade," I told her. I suggested we throw a potluck dinner for the followers of the Bread Exchange in their penthouse on top of the bunker. And so we did. Karen made this lovely daal (lentil dish) for the attendees.

3 cups/600 g dried yellow lentils

½ cup/110 g ghee (clarified butter) or ½ cup/120 ml vegetable oil

4 to 8 fresh chiles (depending on how spicy you like it), stemmed, seeded, and thinly sliced

4 tsp garam masala

1 Tbsp ground cumin (preferably ground in a mortar and pestle)

1 Tbsp turmeric

1 tsp paprika or chili powder

10 cups/2.5 L water, plus more as needed

4 bay leaves

Salt

4 tsp black mustard seeds

2¼ lb/1 kg mixed vegetables, such as green beans, cauliflower, zucchini, carrots, and eggplant, cut into bite-size pieces

Freshly ground pepper

Coconut flakes for garnishing

Chopped fresh cilantro for garnishing

Pappadams or other bread for serving

Put the lentils in a colander, rinse under cold water, and set aside.

In a large stockpot, heat ¼ cup/55 g of the ghee over medium heat. Add the chiles, garam masala, cumin, turmeric, and paprika and cook, stirring, until fragrant. Add the lentils and steam them while stirring. Add the water and 2 of the bay leaves. Cover the pot, turn the heat to low, and let the lentils cook, for 15 to 20 minutes. Check the lentils after 10 minutes and add more water if the daal is too thick and not soupy. Season with salt. Continue cooking until the lentils are cooked through, then remove from the heat and cover to keep warm.

In a large sauté pan or skillet over medium heat, heat the remaining ¼ cup/55 g ghee, add the mustard seeds and remaining 2 bay leaves, cover, and cook until the mustard seeds pop open, approximately 30 seconds. Add the mixed vegetables and briefly sauté them, then add a splash of water to steam the vegetables for about 5 minutes, or just until they soften. Season with salt and pepper.

Serve the daal in a large bowl with the vegetables spooned on top. Garnish with the coconut flakes and cilantro. Serve the pappadams alongside.

>> Since this recipe is an inherently healthy dish, I like to maximize its healthfulness by buying organic ingredients.

>> You can prepare the lentils and vegetables a day ahead, but make sure to cook both al dente, so neither one becomes too soft when you assemble and heat the dish for serving.

>> Depending on how spicy you like your daal, you can use fewer chiles. I used eight.

Meine Reise zu gutem Fleisch begann am gleichen Tag
wie meine Freundschaft zu Malin. Noch besser gesagt:
Sie war die Reiseleiterin. Sie stellte mir das Visum aus für
eine neue kulinarische Welt. Es war im Sommer 2010.
Alle waren im Fußballfieber. 300 leute. Auf der Sonnen-
terrasse des Soho House in Berlin-Mitte waren es 30°C
und alle klebten an die großen Leinwände.

Mich beschäftigte mehr der sich leerende Longdrink in meiner
Hand als das Spiel, als auf einmal eine gutaussehende Blondine
geradewegs auf mich zukam. Ich kannte sie flüchtig, weil ihr
Exfreund und meine Exfreundin mal was miteinander hatten. Sie
baute sich vor mir auf: "Conrad, ich habe ein Problem. Alle meine
Freundinnen sind Vegetarier. Du magst doch Fleisch? Du kochst
doch gern, oder?"

Von mir kamen ein kurzes: "Ja." und "Ja."

"Ich möchte morgen einen Grillkurs machen. Hast du Lust?",
fragte sie mich.

Lange Rede, kurzer Sinn: Am nächsten Tag grillten wir 14 Sorten Fleisch, hörten
stundenlange Vorträge über Tierrassen, Temperaturen, Fett als Geschmacksträger,
Geduld, Zeit und das richtige Timing beim Zubereiten von Fleisch und erfuhren viel
über die Unsitte, es aus mangelndem Eigengeschmack in Soßen zu ertränken.
Die wichtigste Grundregel, die wir lernten: Weniger ist mehr! Feuer, Fleisch – und gut
ist. Zuletzt mussten wir das Versprechen ablegen, nie wieder Filet zu bestellen. Das sei
langweiliges Fleisch ohne Fett – also ohne Geschmack. Zugegeben, hin und wieder
habe ich dieses Versprechen gebrochen.

Mir eröffneten sich nach diesem Kurs ganz neue Horizonte.
Auf den Grillkurs folgten Niedergarkurse und Experimente mit anderen
Fleischsorten. Mein Favorit ist und bleibt ein Dry Aged Entrecote vom
Hereford-Rind. Dieses Gericht habe ich auch gewählt, als ich Malin
bekochte. Ein englisches vier Kilogramm schweres Steak aus Hereford
kämpfte an diesem Tag gegen einen schlanken drei Kilogramm
schweren Wagyū, ein exklusives japanisches Rind. In 2,5 x 2,5 cm große
Würfel geschnitten, mit frisch gemahlenem Pfeffer, Meersalz und dem
besten Olivenöl ins Fleisch massiert. Beide verbrachten fünf Stunden
im Ofen mit einer finalen fünfminütigen Röstaromen-Kur bei 300°C.
Gewonnen hat mal wieder der Engländer. War mir eigentlich klar. Sie
sind zwar nicht die besten Fußballer, aber gutes Fleisch, das können sie.

—CONRAD FRITZSCH

Stockholm

Crayfish Party in Stockholm, Sweden

You know how some people need to live close to the mountains. And some people need to be close to the open sea. I believe that both places put things in perspective somehow. Nothing is bigger than the sea or a mountain. No person and no building. Sometimes I have the feeling that their greatness helps ensure that nothing, not even ourselves and our own simple lives, can grow too large.

For me, the sea has always kept things in perspective. I grew up by the water and spent every summer on a sailboat with my family. I know that the ocean has the power to calm me down when I am upset. Lying down on the pier, regardless of weather, always soothed any heartache I had as a teenager. It was always comforting that the good spirits and creative flow seemed to return to me when I sat by the water. Somehow water soothes and energizes me at the same time. Maybe salt water is the cure for everything after all. As Karen Blixen wrote in her *Seven Gothic Tales,* the cure-all is "Sweat, or tears, or the salt sea."

I used to be convinced that I couldn't live without a sea breeze in the air to be able to breathe properly, and I would never have thought that I would end up in the German inland, far away from waves and the salty air. Luckily the older I get, distances seem shorter, and every time my life seems to get a bit too large for me to handle, I make a trip to the ocean.

As you can imagine, the things I miss the most about Sweden are the clean water and the smell of fresh fish. Therefore to write a story about the second of the three ingredients in bread, water, I did not have to go very far—I only had to go home.

Because we live so close to the water, seafood has always played a major role in Swedish cooking. I can spend a week at home without eating a single piece of meat. Most of the time at home, I eat shrimp, roe, or fish, whether smoked, cured, or pickled. And then there are the shellfish of all shellfishes: our small lobster look-alikes, the freshwater crayfish.

Crayfish have been part of our food culture in Sweden since the sixteenth century. For decades, they were reserved for aristocracy but, since the mid-nineteenth century, the Swedish aristocracy stopped keeping crayfish to themselves and today these shellfish are one of the country's most beloved delicacies. The crayfish can still be fished out of many of the lakes around the country, like Vättern in Småland, even though it's becoming more difficult to find them.

So when the summer is almost over and the warm, clear evenings are turning darker, the weekends in Sweden turn into large feasts where we, with the help of a lot of schnapps, practically sing praise to the crayfish. They are tiny. In fact, there isn't much meat on them at all. But it doesn't matter. They're still the stars of most Swedish dinners in August.

DALARÖ MACKA (Sandwich from Dalarö Island)
Contributed by Martin Bundock, **SERVES 1**

Martin and I found each other through our work in the fashion business, but we connected because we talked about nothing but food—what we planned to cook, where we'd like to eat, and our latest finds. Since the fashion business can sometimes be a bit like a circus, traveling from one fashion week to the next, we bumped into each other fairly often. Martin would bring me pickled specialties or homemade sausage to exchange for my bread and the jams that I had received through the project.

At a traditional crayfish party, one can get too much to drink before getting a bellyful of food. All those fiddly crayfish never add up to much food when you are also doing shots, so I like to start things off with a simple starter. This is a favorite dish from Sturehof, one of Stockholm's classic restaurants.

Butter the slice of rye bread, and place it on the plate with the two herring fillets on top, side by side.

Sprinkle the chives and onion over the fillets, top with the roe, and form a well in the center.

Carefully place the egg yolk in the well. Place the lemon wedge on the side and grind pepper over the top.

Attack the sandwich, and take your first shot of the crayfish party. It won't be your last.

Salted butter, at room temperature, for spreading

1 thin slice of your favorite rye sourdough bread

2 smoked herring fillets, skin and bones removed

2 Tbsp finely chopped fresh chives

½ red onion, finely chopped

1 Tbsp roe

1 egg yolk

Lemon wedge

Freshly ground pepper

>> The choice of roe is always a personal matter. In Stockholm, the Dalarö sandwich is made with roe from a white fish called *sik*.

CRAIL TAIL

Contributed by Mathin Lundgren, **SERVES 4**

In 1922, Sweden was seriously considering forbidding all alcohol consumption. We pretty much owe it to the crayfish that the law was not enforced. "Kräftor Kräva dessa Drycker" (Crayfish demand these drinks) became the main slogan for keeping alcohol legal. The referendum was a close contest, but with 50.8 percent of the voters, the crayfish won. (Or they lost, depending on how you see it!)

Today, every crayfish dinner with style has its own home-spiced schnapps. To find the best one, I searched the Stockholm night scene and found Mathin, one of Scandinavia's best bartenders. He made me something I had never tried before: the Crail Tail.

3 oz/90 ml spirit vinegar (12% acid)

¾ cup/150 g granulated sugar

1 cup plus 2 tbsp/270 ml water

2 dill crowns

1 lemon

Your favorite vodka, ice cold from the freezer

>> I often freeze my shot glasses, which gives the glass a nice foggy surface when I pour in the vodka.

In a medium saucepan, combine the vinegar, sugar, and water. Bring to a boil over medium-high heat and cook until the sugar has dissolved. Remove the mixture from the heat and let cool slightly. When the mixture has cooled, add the dill. Zest the lemon as meticulously as you can so that no white pith goes into the mixture, and add.

Seal the container and refrigerate overnight.

The next morning, strain the liquid into a nice-looking bottle, add back some of the strained-out dill and zest for decoration, and refrigerate again.

Set the table with eight shot glasses, two per person—one for vodka, one for Crail Tail.

Serve as a double shot: one shot of chilled vodka followed by a shot of Crail Tail.

CRAYFISH FROM SMÅLAND
SERVES 6

My grandfather used to say that when God created the world, He was a bit worried He'd make blunders. So He decided to create the Swedish landscape in Småland, "the Small Country," to freestyle a bit before He got serious. Dark woods and open fields. Deep and shallow lakes. Rocky and sandy coastlines. Everything in one territory. That is why Småland is such a natural beauty (according to my grandfather).

Fill a large stockpot (large enough to hold the crayfish without crowding them but small enough to nest in your largest pot) with water and bring to a boil over high heat. Wash the crayfish in cold water and make sure they are alive, discarding any that are not.

Place the crayfish one at a time into the water, slowly, so that the water stays hot and doesn't stop boiling. The crayfish will quickly turn from black to red. When you've put ten crayfish in the pot and they have all turned red, transfer them from the water to a bowl to dry. Start the process all over again until all forty are cooked and red.

Add the salt, sugar, and paprika to the water and stir well to mix in. Return the cooked crayfish to the pot and place the dill on top, making sure that the crowns are facing downward and submerged in water. I always want my crayfish to have a strong dill taste, so I am never shy about adding lots of it. Turn the heat to low and let the crayfish simmer, not boil, for 10 minutes. Make sure to skim off any foam that might accumulate on the top of the water.

Add the beer to the broth; it will immediately cool down.

Fill a larger pot one-third full with ice-cold water. Nest the stockpot in the pot of cold water to cool it even faster. Once the crayfish are cold, they are ready to be drained and served.

40 crayfish

1¼ cups/210 g salt

¼ cup/50 g granulated sugar

2 Tbsp paprika

2 bunches fresh dill

Two 12-oz/360-ml bottles lager beer

➤➤ If it fits your schedule, boil the crayfish the night before the dinner and let them soak in the stock overnight. They will taste even better.

➤➤ I know how upsetting it is to boil the crayfish alive, but they have to be cooked while still live. When dead, they're just not fresh enough to eat.

VÄSTERBOTTEN QUICHE

Contributed by Mathias Dahlgren, **SERVES 8 TO 10**

On my first visit to Tartine Bakery in San Francisco, I asked baker and co-owner Chad Robertson if he would like me to bring his bread to anyone back home in Europe. He gave me a loaf of a light and juicy sprouted Danish rye bread (see page 222 for the recipe) to bring to great Swedish chef Mathias Dahlgren. So I packed my hand luggage, as I usually do, full of bread, and flew to Stockholm. Later, on his website, Mathias wrote:

> A young woman just visited the Food Bar. She said, "I was in San Francisco yesterday at Tartine, the bakery. They gave me this loaf of bread for you."
>
> Two things are striking. How small the world has become and what a great bread he makes, Chad Robertson.

Since then, Mathias's relaxed Food Bar has been on the top of my list of favorite Swedish restaurants. And now, Mathias has shared a very simple classic Västerbotten Quiche, which is just as mandatory at a crayfish party as the schnapps and the crayfish themselves.

To make the crust: Combine the butter, wheat flour, emmer flour, 1 Tbsp of the water, and the salt in the bowl of a food processor. Blend just until the dough comes together and begins to follow the blade around the bowl, adding the second 1 Tbsp water after the first 10 seconds of blending if the dough appears too dry to come together. Cover the dough and let rest in the refrigerator for at least 1 hour, but not longer than 4 hours.

Preheat the oven to 425°F/220°C. Roll out the crust on a lightly floured work surface into a 10.5-in/26.5-cm round. Transfer the crust to a 9-in/23-cm tart pan with a removable bottom. Prick the base with a fork, line with aluminum foil, fill with dried beans or ceramic pie weights, and bake for about 10 minutes, then lift off the foil and weights and bake for 5 minutes longer, or until golden brown. Set aside the prebaked crust to cool.

To make the filling: First clean the leek, placing the pieces in a small bowl of cold water to wash away the dirt. Change the water three times, or until you no longer see grit and dirt. Drain the leek, chop finely, and transfer to a clean, dry bowl. In a pan over medium heat, melt the butter and then add the leek and gently cook until soft. Let cool until no longer hot to the touch. Whisk the eggs, cream, and sour cream and then add the cheese, cayenne, and leek. Season with salt and black pepper.

Pour the cheese mixture into the crust and bake for about 20 minutes, or until the filling is set in the center when you jiggle the pan. Place the quiche on a cooling rack and cool to room temperature, approximately 2 hours, before you remove it from the pan. Serve at room temperature.

>> In Sweden, we make this quiche in August with a cheese called Västerbotten that originates in the far north, where the nights barely arrive in the summer and the cows graze freely. I was born just a bike ride away from the meadows where the cows roam in the summer, and if there is one Swedish ingredient that I always keep in the refrigerator wherever I am in the world, it is this cheese from West Bothnia. If you cannot get your hands on this cheese, try an aged Gruyère as a substitute.

>> Unlike the crayfish, which we can only get in August, I eat this throughout the whole year.

CRUST

9 Tbsp/125 g butter

1 cup/120 g wheat flour

½ cup/60 g whole emmer flour

1 to 2 Tbsp water (depending on the freshness and quality of the flour)

Pinch of salt

FILLING

1 small leek

1 tsp butter

3 eggs

7 Tbsp/100 ml heavy cream

7 Tbsp/100 ml sour cream or crème fraîche

1¼ cups/150 g grated strong, hard cheese, such as Västerbotten

Pinch of cayenne pepper

Salt and freshly ground black pepper

97 | Stockholm

Bavaria

Brunch in Bavaria, Germany

"What time is it?" he asked.

"It's almost two o'clock," I answered.

"Two is a good time," he said.

I looked down on the melting snow under my hiking boots and smiled.

It was a brilliant thought. Two o'clock really is a good time.

There was still enough time left in this day. Even enough time to start something new

or take a new path. But it was past noon,

and so I was already thinking about the end of the workday.

It had never struck me before. So simple. The revelation was like so many other things I had learned in Bavaria. Sometimes this farmer's-style thinking seemed almost too simple. But when I thought again, it all made sense. It reminded me of my first quarter at Lund University, when I failed my Intellectual History course because I had unnecessarily complicated my line of thinking instead of staying straight and clear. Don't complicate things, Malin, I told myself.

So much knowledge has been captured between the Bavarian mountains. Simple tips and tricks. Awareness that has been passed down through generations. It is easy to make fun of it, the simplicity. The old knowledge. The traditions. *Bauern.* Peasants.

In the southeast corner of Germany, just on the border of Austria, there is a region that honors tradition more than many others. Halfway up the mountain, overlooking Bavaria, you find Rösler Haus. It still belongs to the descendants of German author Jo Hanns Rösler, and it has become the place I go to find space to think and write. The soul of this house is earthy. The first ten seconds on arrival are a more effective stress reduction treatment than any meditation or glass of red wine. I feel it instantly when I arrive and walk around the corner of the house and through the front door. The horizon unfolds in front of me. I take that deep breath. *Ruhe.* Serenity.

With love for every detail, Amely and her mother, Christine, have created a world at Rösler Haus that was unknown to me before I visited them the first time. Whenever I visit, they are dressed in traditional regional folk costumes . . . and practical high-tech sneakers. These ladies seem more cosmopolitan than most of us. I believe that to become a true world citizen, one first needs to be at peace with one's own cultural heritage. And these two women certainly are.

Traditions can be routines that no longer have a primary practical purpose. It is a fine line, this practicing of traditions. It demands an open mind and a high dose of interest and understanding to keep traditions from becoming limiting. When tradition-keepers have an awareness of the changes in society, the traditions can be a way to protect the past from being ruined by modernity. In that sense, I love traditions.

At first, the Rösler Haus seems like any other beautiful farmhouse built in 1685. But if you look closer, there is something special about this place. It is not only the urban flair that grandmother Kitty Rösler brought with her from Vienna (which explains why the bathrooms are decorated as if they were fancy living rooms), it is all the details—the incredible selection of wallpapers, the inviting breakfast table, and the generous fruit tray that reminds me more of a Baroque still life than of something to touch.

I love that Amely decorates my breakfast place setting with blue instead of red because she knows I think it goes better with the farmhouse's interior than the red does. They have a high sensitivity, these women.

I also love their food. The double-baked-crust rye bread from the amazing farmers' market in Munich. The fresh eggs from the neighbors. And the Austrian yogurt and butter. I fill my plate with juniper-smoked ham from the Black Forest, local cheeses, and artisan sausages. I pour elderberry compote over my yogurt. I settle in by the window and let my gaze wander over the mountaintops and the valley below. If I am here in the spring, I carry my plate out the front steps to look down into the valley.

I am the daughter of a sailor. I am not a child of the mountains. But I think I know now what truly connects the mountains and the ocean. The horizon. *Horizontzüchtig*. I am addicted to the horizon.

KITTY'S RÖSLER HAUS ELDERBERRY COMPOTE

Contributed by Christine Schmitt, **MAKES 4 CUPS/1.14 KG**

Compote is best when you use really ripe fruit. Christine from Rösler Haus told me that she usually asks the fruit stand for the fruit that is too old to be sold at the market. Simply remove any damage or dark spots from the fruit and it is good to go. In other words, when the fruit in the fruit bowl is looking saggy, it is time to make compote!

Put the elderberries in a small saucepan and cover with 1 in/2.5 cm of water. Stir in the sugar. Bring to a boil and then turn the heat to low. Simmer for 1 hour, stirring from time to time, making sure that the berries are always covered in water.

Add the whole prunes to the saucepan. (Do not remove the pits from the prunes because they add a lot of flavor to the compote.) Add the cloves and cinnamon stick. Make sure the fruit mix is covered with water and continue to simmer on the lowest heat for 1 hour longer.

While the elderberries and prunes are cooking, peel, core, and quarter the apples and pears. Thinly slice the quarters.

Add the apples, pears, and lemon juice to the simmering fruit mixture, adding more water, if necessary, so that the fruit is always covered with liquid.

Continue to simmer for 30 minutes more or until the fruit is so well cooked through that you cannot tell the different kinds of fruit apart, which is what I like so much about Kitty's compote!

Taste for sweetness, and stir in more sugar until the compote is as sweet as you like. Remove the prune pits. Serve or cover tightly and store in the refrigerator for up to 10 days.

1 lb/455 g elderberries, fresh or frozen

¼ cup/50 g granulated sugar, plus more for sweetening

12 whole fresh prunes, stemmed

2 whole cloves

One ½-in-/1-cm-long piece cinnamon stick

2 apples

2 pears

Juice of 1 lemon

>> The amount of sugar used in the compote is an individual choice. The sweetness of your compote also depends on the ripeness of the fruit. The riper the fruit, the sweeter your compote will be. Very ripe fruit might only need 3 Tbsp of sugar, and less ripe fruit might call for much more.

BLOOD ORANGE CURD WITH ROSEMARY

Contributed by Sasha Gora, **MAKES 1 CUP/270 G**

With winter comes citrus season. As both the snow and your layers of socks build up, citrus season almost feels like nature's way of saying, "Hang in there." This blood orange curd with rosemary celebrates the arrival of citrus season in the midst of winter. It is bright and cheerful and fresh, a taste of spring to come. Curd is most commonly made with lemons. Made with blood oranges, it is a little sweeter and the rosemary adds more depth of flavor. Although blood oranges are certainly sweeter than lemons, they still have that refreshing citrus tang that is preserved so well in the curd.

2 blood oranges

1 cup/200 g granulated sugar

6 fresh rosemary sprigs

1 tbsp fresh lemon juice

2 eggs plus 2 egg yolks

6 Tbsp/85 g unsalted butter

>> Since this recipe calls for zest, it really is best to use organic, unwaxed oranges. If you have trouble finding organic ones, simply remove the wax from the oranges by placing them in a pot of boiling water for a minute or two and then giving them a good scrub.

>> You shouldn't have any problems with the eggs cooking while you are making the curd if you keep the pot of simmering water at a low enough temperature. However, if the temperature gets a bit too hot and you end up with a few cooked lumps of eggs, simply strain the curd before it cools.

Zest the oranges and reserve the zest in plastic wrap. Juice the oranges to make about 1 cup/250 ml juice. Strain the juice into a small saucepan over medium heat and bring to a simmer. Let the juice simmer until it reduces by one-third, which will concentrate and deepen the flavor. Add the sugar and stir until the sugar dissolves completely. Remove the pan from the heat, add the rosemary sprigs, and cover. Leave to infuse for 1 hour.

Discard the rosemary and add the blood orange zest and lemon juice.

In a small bowl, lightly beat the eggs and egg yolks and set aside.

Fill a small saucepan one-third full with water and then bring to a gentle simmer over low heat.

While the water heats, cut the butter into small cubes and place in a medium-size heatproof bowl (such as a stainless-steel mixing bowl). Add the juice mixture.

Once the water is simmering, place the bowl on top of the saucepan to make a double boiler. With a wooden spoon, stir the butter and juice mixture occasionally until the butter melts. Once the butter has melted, add the eggs and stir constantly. Check the water to make sure it is barely simmering; any hotter and it could overheat the curd, cooking the eggs before the curd is cooked. Stir for about 10 minutes or until the curd coats the back of the wooden spoon. The consistency should be comparable to melted ice cream and the temperature should be about 166°F/75°C. Remove from the heat and stir occasionally as it cools. The curd will thicken as it cools.

Once cool, transfer the curd to a jar with a lid and store in the refrigerator for up to 2 weeks. Make sure to use a clean spoon each time you scoop it out to ensure that it lasts longer!

PEAR AND GINGER JAM

Contributed by Sasha Gora, **MAKES 2 CUPS/570 G**

Unlike the blood orange curd with rosemary, this pear and ginger jam captures the other side of winter—cozy, warm, and dark. It satisfies cravings for spice and hearty flavors and captures that winter urge to curl up under a wool blanket and watch the snowfall. This jam is chunky and thick— a cross between a thick fruit compote with bits of fruit and a smooth fruit sauce—which makes it just as good stirred into a bowl of hot oatmeal as it is spread on a piece of toasted sourdough with a slice of aged Cheddar.

In a wide, heavy-bottomed pot, combine the pears with the sugar, lemon juice, and ginger. Split the vanilla bean, scrape the seeds into the pot, add the scraped-out pod to the pot, and set aside to macerate for 15 minutes. Put a small plate or saucer in the freezer (to use later for testing the jam's readiness).

Bring the pears to a boil over medium-high heat. Stir occasionally and cook until the fruit begins to fall apart and it is possible to mash the pears with the back of a wooden spoon. Remove the pot from the stove, discard the vanilla bean pod, and use a potato masher to mash the pears. Return the pot to the stove and continue to cook over low heat until the mixture reaches the consistency of jam.

To test whether the jam is done, remove the plate from the freezer and spoon a small amount of jam onto it. Let the jam sit for a minute or two and then check to see if the jam has become firm. The jam won't gel, but it will firm up. If the jam is still quite liquid, continue to cook it, repeating the cold plate test until it passes.

With a ladle, fill some clean lidded jam jars with the hot jam, making sure to leave a bit of headspace at the top.

Wipe the rims of the jars with a wet paper towel to catch any drops of jam. Place the lids on the jars and screw on the rings. Set aside to cool. When completely cool, store in the refrigerator and use the jam within 2 weeks.

3 lb/1.36 kg pears, peeled, cored, and diced

1½ cups/300 g granulated sugar

¼ cup/60 ml fresh lemon juice

3 Tbsp peeled and finely grated fresh ginger

1 vanilla bean

>> Use whichever pears you like best or are easiest to find. At Rösler Haus, Sasha used Bartlett pears. If they are organic, you can certainly pass on peeling them.

BIRCHER MUESLI

MAKES ABOUT 4 CUPS/900 G

My German friend Fee is of Greek heritage. When her grandmother cooked for her family, she always placed the meal on the table and said, "This meal I cooked with the love I feel for you." When the food had not turned out as she had expected, this was a very effective preamble. No one ever complained.

Regardless of how tired I have been in the morning, I have never failed to make Bircher Muesli. But if anyone complains about the look of the breakfast you make early in the morning, just remember to quote Fee's grandmother.

Using a box grater set over a large bowl, coarsely grate the apples. Add the coconut water, ¼ cup/60 ml of the yogurt, the oats, goji berries, flaxseed, and mint to the bowl and stir until thoroughly combined.

Cover the muesli and refrigerate overnight.

The next morning, mix the remaining 1 cup/240 ml yogurt, the maple syrup, and salt into the muesli and spoon into bowls. Garnish as desired before serving.

2 apples, such as Granny Smith, peeled and cored

1¼ cups/300 ml coconut water

1¼ cups/300 ml plain Greek yogurt (3.5 percent fat or more)

1 cup/250 g rolled oats, kamut, or spelt

¾ cup/85 g dried goji berries

3 Tbsp flaxseed

2 Tbsp coarsely chopped fresh mint leaves

3 Tbsp maple syrup

Pinch of salt

Fresh berries, mint leaves, granola, Cape gooseberries, and chopped nuts, for garnishing (optional)

>> The muesli can be prepared ahead and refrigerated for up to 3 days.

>> I use coconut water and not whole milk, so I prefer to use a yogurt with a fairly high fat percentage (between 3.5 percent and 10 percent fat).

DOLL FAMILY BREAD SPREADS
Contributed by Ingrid Doll

Imagine having a mother who loves high-quality cheeses and fine wines and who runs a delicacy store. Imagine receiving weekly care packages filled with goodies like artisan chocolate and locally produced truffled salumi. And then imagine being vegetarian. And a closeted one, because you simply do not want to disappoint your mom.

This is the story of how I met Stefanie Doll in 2009. With a refrigerator filled with homemade sausages and cold cuts, she offered to trade bread for anything her mother, Ingrid, sent that she could not eat. A win–win situation.

HAM AND CHIVE SALAD
MAKES 1½ CUPS/770 G

1 lb/455 g cooked ham, diced

2 bunches fresh chives, chopped

1 cup/250 g mayonnaise

¼ cup/60 ml pickling liquid from your favorite pickles

2 Tbsp whole milk

Salt and freshly ground pepper

In a small bowl, mix the ham together with the chives. In a medium bowl, whisk the mayonnaise, pickling liquid, and milk until smooth. Add to the ham-chive mixture and gently fold in. Season with salt and pepper.

Store the spread, covered, in the refrigerator for up to 3 days.

≫ Cooked and cured ham is already salty, so I usually skip the salt and find that a couple of rough grinds with the pepper mill is enough.

DOLLS' CREAM CHEESE
MAKES ½ CUP/560 G

12 oz/500 g cream cheese

¼ cup/60 ml milk

2 young carrots, thinly sliced

2 green onions, white and green parts, thinly sliced

Handful chopped fresh chives

Handful chopped fresh parsley

Salt and freshly ground pepper

1 garlic clove, minced (optional)

In a medium bowl, whisk the cream cheese with the milk until smooth. Stir in the carrots, green onions, chives, and parsley. Season with salt and pepper. Stir in the garlic (if using) and serve.

Store the spread, covered, in the refrigerator for up to 3 days.

SCHMALZNUDELN (Schmaltz Fritters)

Contributed by Nicky Stich, **MAKES ABOUT 15 FRITTERS**

If you are having a really late night out in Munich and feel like a snack before you go to bed, a visit in the early morning hours to the city's traditional Schmalznudel maker is mandatory.

Nicky introduced me to these doughnut-like pastries the first time we met in Munich when, in exchange for bread, she showed me her secret food spots in the city. Over Schmalznudeln at the farmers' market in Munich, we talked about how everything, from wine to the smallest ingredients, needs a story to really engage us. As we spoke, the pastries landed on our plates fresh out of the oil and dipped in sugar. In Bavarian homes, the Schmalznudeln are made for carnival in February and garnished with a puff of powdered sugar.

In a small saucepan, melt the 6 tbsp/85 g butter over low heat, then remove from the heat and let cool. Pour the flour into a large bowl or the bowl of a stand mixer and make a well in the center. Crumble the yeast into it, then pour ⅓ cup/80 ml of the milk over it. Stir once, then cover the bowl and let rest in a warm spot for 15 to 20 minutes, or until bubbles form.

Add the remaining ⅓ cup/80 ml milk, the sugar, salt, eggs, and ¼ cup/55 g of the melted butter and mix well to incorporate. If the dough is dry, add milk, 1 Tbsp at a time, until the dough holds together enough to knead. Knead thoroughly by hand or with the mixer's dough hook until the dough is shiny and barely sticky. Divide the dough into fifteen pieces, shaping each one into a neat ball. Brush the balls lightly with more melted butter. Place on a baking sheet, cover, and let rise for another 15 to 20 minutes.

Fill a deep fryer or large saucepan with the clarified butter to a depth of at least 3 in/8 cm and heat over high heat to 345°F/175°C. Rub your fingers with butter and finish shaping the fritters. Carefully stretch each dough ball into a disk, pulling from the center so it is thin in the middle and forms an even, thick edge (as thick as your index finger).

Carefully put a couple of the dough disks into the hot butter and immediately spoon some fat over them—this helps to develop their characteristic shape. When the bottoms have turned golden brown, turn them over and fry until both sides are golden brown. As you fry the second side, make sure no butter pools in the center of the disks, which can ruin their light texture on the inside. Drain on paper towels and dust with powdered sugar, then serve.

6 Tbsp/85 g butter, plus 2 lb/910 g, clarified, for deep-frying

4 cups/500 g organic unbleached all-purpose flour

2 Tbsp/20 g fresh cake yeast

⅔ cup/160 ml lukewarm (105°F/40°C) milk, plus more as needed

Generous ⅓ cup/75 g superfine sugar

Pinch of salt

2 eggs

Powdered sugar for dusting

➤➤ For a hint of cinnamon on your fritters, mix 1 tsp ground cinnamon with the powdered sugar before dusting.

Sour Soups for Chilly Days in Warsaw, Poland

When I arrived in Warsaw for the first time in 2007, I had a flashback memory of my first impression of Berlin seven years earlier; the smell of charcoal that heated the apartments and the dirty gray color of concrete. I had taken the night train from Berlin and arrived at six-thirty in the morning. I remember taking a taxi to the fancy hotel my employer had booked. The breakfast included everything from caviar to Champagne and Polish vodka.

Just like Berlin, the city felt eager to achieve something. Unlike designers in Germany or Sweden, the young Warsaw designers had well-functioning, local production that they took advantage of. Everything looked promising. I had traveled to Warsaw to work with the guerilla store Comme des Garçons, and the fashion scene seemed to be bubbling. I got to know Robert Serek, a Krakow-born mathematician, who was building stores in unrenovated buildings in a way that had never been seen before. Looking back on the trips I made during that time, I always end up thinking of the lovely evenings with friends at U Kucharzy, a restaurant whose name translates to "dinner by the chefs" or chef's dinner.

When I was planning out where to travel and trade with the Bread Exchange for this book, I realized I should visit another city to balance the scenic stories I was gathering from the countryside. In the end, I am a city girl and the Bread Exchange has been a project that mainly takes place in cities. I decided to choose a lesser-known city that I had a personal connection to. I thought about upcoming food trends. I saw how the interest in sausage making in Sweden was rising, and I had been to San Francisco and seen that Bar Tartine was cooking dishes that reminded me of Eastern Europe. Another food trend, fermented vegetables, which I personally love, is a large part of Polish food heritage. The common denominator seemed to be Poland. As the largest city in this former Eastern Bloc country, and one with a rapidly changing society, Warsaw had a story to tell. I knew I would not be the only one who was curious about Poland's food culture.

In 2013, I returned, with a completely different goal than I had on my previous trips for work: I wanted to check out what was happening in food (not fashion) in Warsaw. After the collapse of Communism in 1989, the growing middle class seemed eager to sink their teeth into Poland's somewhat slumbering food culture. After a short period of pseudo-French trends in Warsaw, the spotlight is now on Polish traditional cuisine. Young chefs make modern interpretations and research heirloom vegetable varieties, and family-run farms thrive in every corner of the country.

In the past year, great food magazines also began popping up in Poland. They do it well, the Polish people. Poland has a long history of great illustrators, and today impressive graphic designers and creative artists abound. The interest in food is rising everywhere but, still, I was baffled by how fast it seemed to be growing in Warsaw. I asked everyone I met why. Why are the Polish people willing to spend three times more on food than Americans do, and almost double what Germans spend? There seemed to be as many reasons as people I met. Polish people have a history of enjoying dinners together, something that is not uncommon in countries where the family, and also the church, play such an important role. Agriculture has always played an important part in the Polish economy and almost 60 percent of the land is cultivated. But, unlike its Eastern Bloc neighbors during the Communist era, whose farms were turned into large state-owned, factory-like estates, most of the Polish farms remained privately owned. When the borders opened in 1989, Poland still had a fairly classic food production system to return to.

Political journalist Anne Applebaum described the Polish countryside as a part of Europe that is "still a little bit wilder, a little bit less well-groomed, and a little bit more primitive than the countryside in the lands to the West." I like that. And I really like that the Polish people are so proud of this.

As I returned to Warsaw, almost six years after my previous visit, the energy felt the same but the focus was different. The food scene in the city was boiling. Several new small restaurants were serving classic dishes, complete with waiters eager to tell the story of the ingredients in the dishes. The bread was a door opener that, once again, invited me into people's homes. I felt their pride as they talked about their love of their land, food, and locally grown ingredients. We talked about grandmothers' pickled cucumbers. And the amazing variety of apples that you could find in the countryside. And we ate soup. Lots of soup.

My trip to Warsaw took place in the ice-cold month of February, when the days are dark and the cold wind sneaks under your shirt. It is soup season. Polish people know this well. With a winter that can be as rough as concrete, Poland has developed a culinary culture jammed with interesting and strengthening soups. I have picked out three of my favorites for the winter season. The common thread is the sour note that runs through all of them. Because fresh ingredients are limited in the winter, they use a lot of pickled and fermented vegetables, and also horseradish, which I learned is important in every Polish family's home.

ZALEWAJKA NA MAŚLANCE Z CHRZANOWYM PURÉE
(Buttermilk Soup with Horseradish Mashed Potatoes)
Contributed by Jakub Jezierski, SERVES 6

Someone once said that making your own stock is something for people with too much time or an overly developed self-image. This was also my opinion—until I made stock myself. Making stock is not only a way to help you feel a little bit better, it is also a great way of using up of vegetables and trimmings destined for the compost. Anything you planned to throw away goes into the stockpot. Pick out anything droopy in the veggie bin and use the green tops of the leek that you would have otherwise thrown away. If you don't have a compost bucket standing around, just keep a bag of veggie scraps in the freezer. When the bag is full, it is time to make stock. Making your own stock does not cost you anything more than the energy to cook it. But the best reason to make your own stock is that it will take all the soups in this chapter to the next level.

BUTTERMILK SOUP

8 cups/2 L good-quality beef or vegetable stock

4 cups/1 L buttermilk

¼ cup/30 g organic unbleached all-purpose flour

4 garlic cloves, minced

2 tsp caraway seeds

Salt

6 slices thick-cut bacon

HORSERADISH MASHED POTATOES

Salt

2½ lb/1.2 kg baking potatoes (preferably with skins left on), quartered

½ cup/120 ml milk

3 Tbsp butter

2 Tbsp grated horseradish

Freshly ground pepper

To make the buttermilk soup: In a large saucepan, heat the stock over medium heat until simmering.

In a medium bowl, mix the buttermilk, flour, and garlic. Whisk the buttermilk-flour mixture into the warm stock and stir in the caraway seeds. Simmer for 5 to 10 minutes. Do not let the mixture boil or the buttermilk may separate. Season with salt. Keep the soup warm while you cook the bacon.

In a frying pan over medium-high heat, cook the bacon until crisp. Transfer the bacon to a plate lined with paper towels and blot away grease. Cut the strips in half and set aside.

To make the mashed potatoes: Fill a large stockpot halfway with water and bring to a boil over high heat. Add a few pinches of salt. Add the potatoes and boil until tender. While the potatoes are cooking, in a small saucepan, warm the milk and butter over low heat until the butter is melted and the milk is hot but not boiling. Drain the potatoes and return them to the stockpot, then add the horseradish and the milk mixture a little at a time and coarsely mash with a potato masher or a fork. (You do not want the mash to be too liquidy because it is served in the soup.) Taste and season with salt and pepper.

Ladle the soup into serving bowls. Spoon a mound of mashed potatoes into the middle of the soup, garnish with a bacon slice, and serve.

>> I leave the peels on the potatoes because I like the texture and the look of peel in the mash.

ŻUREK ALBO "BARSZCZ BIALY" (Sour Bread Soup, or White Barszcz)
Contributed by Anne Applebaum, SERVES 4 TO 6

I can't help but wonder how this soup came to be in the first place. How does one get the idea to add a smelly, fermented liquid to the Easter soup? To me, it sounded like a plot to poison someone! Despite my initial thoughts when I learned how this soup is made, it has turned out to be one of my favorites. Like sushi, I don't think I could ever get tired of it.

Foreign correspondent and author Anne Applebaum explains this soup best in her own words:

In its way, żurek is the most humble and most exotic of all Polish soups, at least to the foreign palate. It is traditionally eaten at Easter, but now is found on menus all year-round. Though distantly related to the bread and garlic soups of Spain and Italy, its base is not meat or vegetable broth, but a fermented liquid called zakwas.

Zakwas, which is, in turn, distantly related both to sourdough and to Russian kvass, a fermented, mildly alcoholic drink, is made from rye bread and water. In Poland, zakwas is available in bottles at ordinary supermarkets. Outside of Poland, you can find it in specialty ethnic markets, and even online. Although it sounds odd and intimidating, it is in fact extremely easy to make, but it does require planning a few days in advance.

Żurek can be thin and delicate or hearty and stuffed with chunks of ham, sausage, and potatoes—in which case it is really an entire meal. The Easter version always contains biała kielbasa, or spicy white sausage (similar to bratwurst). Sometimes żurek, like its Italian cousin, zuppa di pan cotto, is served with hard-boiled egg. But it is always sour, salty, and creamy at the same time, which makes it unlike almost anything else.

And, of course, its taste is almost mystically linked to the sour bread in its broth. On the drive from Warsaw to our country house near Bydgoszcz, my family often stops at a roadside restaurant that serves żurek in a "bowl" made from a scooped-out loaf of brown bread. In its way, this is the perfect combination: you drink your soup, then eat the bread which has already lent its essence to the soup.

Once you've tried it, the taste of żurek stays with you. It's the one thing that I always recommend to foreigners visiting Poland for the first time, since they can't get anything quite like it anywhere else. Over the years I've met a number of Japanese people who have been to Poland (there are more than you might imagine, such is the pull of Chopin's birthplace). Almost every single one of them specifically mentioned żurek as the one Polish food he or she could never forget. Perhaps there is some link between sour bread soup and sushi; I leave that for others to interpret.

The version served here is similar to one in my cookbook, From a Polish Country House Kitchen. It is on the lighter side, and cheats somewhat by adding vegetable broth, instead of water, during the cooking process. I also like the spiciness of the horseradish and, perhaps for similar reasons, I prefer sausage to egg.

Use Polish biala kielbasa or bratwurst if you can get it, but if not, there are many lightly spiced chicken, veal, or pork sausages that would work. They don't have to be precooked, as they will be boiled in the soup.

To make the zakwas: Put the water, bread crusts, flour, and garlic in an extra-large storage jar with a screw-on lid. Leave the jar in a warm place—on a windowsill or in a cupboard—for 4 to 5 days. Open the jar, remove any mold or green bits that might have accumulated on top, and strain. The remaining sour, fermented liquid is the zakwas. Measure out 2 cups/480 ml for the soup and set aside. The remaining zakwas can be stored in the jar in the refrigerator for up to 2 weeks.

In a large saucepan, combine the water, onion halves, carrot, parsnip, and celery root and bring to a boil over high heat. Turn the heat to low and simmer, uncovered, for 40 minutes or so. Strain the broth and discard the vegetables.

Meanwhile, in a stockpot, sauté together the chopped onion, garlic, bacon, and sausage over medium-high heat until all are lightly browned. Add the strained vegetable broth, horseradish, marjoram, peppercorns, allspice, and bay leaf. Bring to a boil, turn the heat to low, and cook at a low boil for 20 minutes. Stir in the 2 cups/480 ml zakwas and the cream. Increase the heat to medium-high, and bring to a boil again. Remove the bay leaf and serve with bread, if desired, on the side.

ZAKWAS

2 cups/480 ml warm water

1 cup/225 g rye bread crusts

½ cup/60 g rye flour

2 garlic cloves, minced

6 cups/1.4 L water

2 onions, peeled, one halved and one coarsely chopped

1 carrot, peeled

1 parsnip, peeled

½ celery root, peeled

2 garlic cloves, finely chopped

4 strips bacon, cooked and chopped

2¼ lb/570 g white sausage, cut into chunks

¼ cup/55 g grated white horseradish

1 Tbsp dried marjoram

6 peppercorns

3 allspice berries

1 bay leaf

½ cup/120 ml light cream

Crusty brown bread for serving (optional)

V
Yuncta potatoes harvested
of July after a
have enabled us to
notes of apple.
and a hint of citrus
out vintage.
bottles
500ml

ZUPA OGORKOWA (Polish Sour Cucumber Soup with Dill)

Contributed by Robert Serek, **SERVES 4**

On my first visit to Warsaw in 2007, Robert invited me to dinner at U Kucharzy, a restaurant that occupies the kitchen of one of Warsaw's two former Communist-era hotels. In fact, the restaurant was located in the middle of the old kitchen.

That evening, I experienced something I had never seen before. The guests in the restaurant were seated in the midst of the chefs' kitchen. The steam from the soup pots added mystique to the experience. We could observe how the food was created for all the tables in the restaurant. We could follow the staff's well-choreographed performance.

Some of the dishes were made at the table. I had never seen a beef tartare cut so precisely as by the young man in charge of it. The baker, an older woman with a grandmotherly smile, brought in a wagon of homemade cakes for us to choose from. On my first visit, I listened to the stories of the local farms that had produced everything from beef to butter to snap peas and how the game meat we had enjoyed had been hunted. Looking back, I realize that this dinner in Warsaw was my first true farm-to-table experience.

Fill a large stockpot with the water. Add the chicken wings, bring to a simmer over low heat, and simmer, uncovered, for at least 30 minutes, or up to 4 hours. Skim any foam off of the surface.

While the stock is simmering, wash the leek. Cut off all but about 1 in/2.5 cm of the green, cut the leek in half and place in a bowl of cold water, sloshing the pieces around to wash away any dirt. Drain, add fresh water, and repeat. Change the water and repeat until you no longer see grit and dirt in the water.

Add the leek, celery root, 1 carrot, and 1 parsley root to the stock and simmer for another 30 minutes. Pour the stock through a strainer into another stockpot. Discard the vegetables and reserve the chicken for another use. If you want a richer stock, simmer the stock for 20 minutes longer. Meanwhile, bring a stockpot of salted water to boil. Add the potatoes and cook for 20 minutes.

Melt the butter in a medium sauté pan or skillet over medium-low heat; add the pickles, remaining carrot, and remaining parsley root; and sauté for 10 minutes. You still want to make sure not to cook the vegetables too long. Transfer the mixture to a stockpot. Add the stock, allspice, bay leaves, and pickling liquid. Taste and add more pickling liquid or salt, if desired. The soup should have a pleasantly sour taste.

Ladle the soup into a tureen or individual bowls and serve with a sprinkling of dill. Serve the sour cream at the table for everyone to spoon into their soup. Or decorate each bowl with the sour cream and let your guests stir it in.

6 cups/1.4 L water or chicken or vegetable broth

6 chicken wings and/or legs, skin left on

1 leek

1 celery root, halved

2 carrots, peeled and diced

2 parsley roots, cut into ½-in/12-mm pieces

5 potatoes, peeled and diced

1 Tbsp butter

6 dill pickles, coarsely grated, plus ¾ cup/ 180 ml dill pickling liquid

4 allspice berries

4 bay leaves

Salt (optional)

Chopped fresh dill for garnishing

7 oz/200 g sour cream

A Rooftop Afternoon in Brooklyn, New York

Everything simply tastes clearer, sweeter, bolder, and crisper when you take the time to really experience it. Sharing food is an expression of love and self-respect. Through food I give love, not only to others but also to myself. When I feel good in body and mind, I taste everything in a completely different way and I take the time to enjoy it.

But food can also be a double-edged sword. Just as eating is one way of taking care of oneself, it can also be a mode of controlled self-destruction, which can be addictive and terribly hard to shed. I have loved working in the fashion business but I have also become used to being surrounded by people who forgot the importance of treating themselves with respect and enjoying food. To lose the ability to enjoy food is a punishment I do not wish on my worst enemy. Not eating is practically the same as not respecting yourself. Don't get me wrong; there are many people with a healthy sense of self in the fashion industry. However, there is a difference between centering on one's self and having enough confidence to focus on others.

To truly love those around us, we need to start by loving ourselves. The food we make and share is an expression of how we feel about ourselves and how we relate to others. It should not be surprising that my closest friends over the years have shared my love for food.

Even in a superficial industry, I have collected a group of girlfriends who know how to treat themselves as well as the people around them. And this chapter is dedicated to them. And to New York City.

It sounds clichéd, but I have never visited another place on this planet that makes my heart pound as fast as New York City. Despite the overseas flight, the jet lag, and even the hassle of customs and passport controls—when I am sitting in a cab pointed toward Manhattan, I can do nothing but smile. My stomach tends to bubble like carbonated water and somewhere behind where my heart lies, the butterflies mutate into prehistoric pterodactyls.

I have never stayed in New York City long enough to experience the financial challenges of living there. For me, it is the place that gets me to be my best. And it is certainly a place that inspires me. The city makes me move faster, but at the same time feel more relaxed than ever.

One thing that always strikes me in New York City is the women. There is that certain kind of New York lady who has an impressively thick skin. The ones who have also managed to keep warmth in their hearts are the kind that truly inspire me.

I decided to do Bread Exchange in New York because I wanted to capture the spirit of what I love about the city and its women. I went in early October and invited the so-called good ladies of NYC. Since I do not know all of the good ladies personally, I asked some of my dearest friends around the world who they would invite if they were me. I wanted to have a nice mix of creative women who are not afraid to share their networks and who believe that helping others is not something you do to accrue karma, but that it is fun and rewarding. I would call them ladies with strong arms but not dirty elbows. In other words, ladies who enjoy life. And that includes ladies who know how to enjoy food.

All I brought in my suitcase, apart from the usual six pairs of shoes and enough outfits to suit every possible mood and spontaneous party, was a kitchen scale, some Japanese charcoal received in trade, and my sourdough starter. I had no idea where I would bake. I had no photographer. All I knew was that Gina Hamadey from *Food & Wine* magazine was willing to let me borrow her Brooklyn rooftop on one Sunday afternoon.

Just like the city itself, the weather in New York can be extreme. On Wednesday it was clear, but the worst weather possible was forecasted for Sunday, the day of the rooftop gathering. The first autumn day would bring rain and cold winds. I wondered whether I should cancel and try again in the spring. Friday, however, was expected to be the perfect Indian summer day. But Friday was only twenty-six hours away. There were so many details to sort out—all in such a short period of time.

I sat on my bed at the Gramercy Park Hotel with my friend Nancy Bachmann from Los Angeles, discussing the situation while the sourdough starter was flooding the minibar (out of excitement, no doubt).

A last-minute cancellation was not an option. There were so many people involved and, at that point, more than twenty women were coming. Kari Morris, Brooklyn's master of syrups and shrubs, was going to make drinks; Ira Chernova and Kate Cunningham, to whom I had just been introduced, had offered to help with photography; Katharina Riess from Friends of Truths-Network had sent me her amazing pinot grigio; Linda Niklasson had flown in from Stockholm to make the perfect burger; and my friend Nancy just happened to be in town.

So I decided to run with it and, from that point on, everything flowed. It was as though the spirit of Indian summer blew energy and warm winds to propel me along. I hoped that we could just make the best of it. And we did.

Annabelle, from *Vanity Fair,* whom I'd never met before, had read the call-for-help post on my blog and called to offer assistance. "Do you have a budget?" she asked, "No, no budget," I answered, adding, "I can trade for bread and an afternoon with some of the best girls in New York City." Within two hours she had pulled some strings and arranged for flower stylist Taylor Patterson to help out. Nicole Salazar, who just one year earlier in Berlin had traded her copy of Patti Smith's autobiography for a loaf of my bread, had confirmed and offered to bring her grandmother's Cheese Phyllo Squares (page 65). My friend Vili Petrova and Kate Cunningham, one of the friends of a friend I had never met before, ran around Manhattan to get film for the cameras. Nancy made sure the wine arrived at the ideal temperature. Nhung Nguyen closed her store early and went home to bake chocolate chip cookies to solve my no-dessert dilemma.

I went out onto the street in Soho in search for someone willing to let me borrow an oven for an hour. I went to the beautiful delicacy store Russ & Daughters on Houston Street to ask for help. People who know quality are usually a good place to start because they understand why someone would twist an arm to stick to the ideal. As I explained my mission over the salmon-filled counter, a Swiss guy in line behind me must have overheard the conversation. He said, "You can use the oven at my restaurant if you like." I asked him if he thought that his oven would be good enough for what I was doing, saying, "I need it to be really hot, like 550 degrees Fahrenheit." He answered that he thought it would work, since he used it for making focaccia, too. He gave me his number and we agreed that I would come by later. And that is the story of how I ended up baking my bread for that afternoon's party at chef Daniel Humm's restaurant, NoMad. It is open-minded people like these who make the world—and the Bread Exchange—so special.

In the end, the afternoon did not turn out picture-perfect. But to me it was exactly how it should be. I think that the way this October afternoon came together paints the perfect picture of the people who inspire me, and what I love about New York City. It showed me one of its great contrasts: How even in the busiest city in the world, among all that hustle and bustle, people surprise you. Without hesitating, they take time to slow down, enjoy, and help. The city might give you strong winds and rain when you plan to feast outside, but the same city gives you a summer day in the middle of fall and delivers the type of people who show up no matter what. It also shows how nothing can be done without the help of others.

HIBISCUS-GINGER COCKTAIL AND CONCORD SPRITZER COCKTAIL

Contributed by Kari Morris

The colors of these drinks perfectly matched the early fall season—deep purple and warm yellow—the day we gathered. I had never met Kari Morris until she set up her beautiful cocktail still life on the New York City rooftop. We were introduced by a mutual friend from Berlin. On extremely short notice, Kari pulled strings and arranged everything, from glassware to goody bags. She is a businesswoman with good energy. A real inspiration.

HIBISCUS-GINGER COCKTAIL
SERVES 4

2 cups/480 ml filtered water

½ cup/30 g dried hibiscus flowers

1½ oz/45 ml rum

¾ oz/20 ml ginger syrup

½ oz/15 ml fresh lemon juice

Crushed ice

Bring the filtered water to a boil. Steep the hibiscus in the hot water until cool. Strain out the flowers. Add the hibiscus water, rum, ginger syrup, and lemon juice to a cocktail shaker with crushed ice. Shake and strain into coupe glasses and serve.

≫ The hibiscus water can be stored in a glass container, covered, in the refrigerator for up to 1 week.

CONCORD SPRITZER COCKTAIL
SERVES 1

5 Concord grapes

1½ oz/45 ml vodka

½ oz/15 ml ginger syrup

½ oz/15 ml fresh lemon juice

Ice cubes

Splash of seltzer water

Muddle the grapes in a cocktail shaker. Add the vodka, ginger syrup, and lemon juice. Add ice to the shaker, shake well, strain, and pour over fresh ice cubes in a highball glass. Top off with the seltzer water before serving.

≫ Kari chose Concord grapes that are grown locally in upstate New York. The powdery white bloom that covers this grape adds a beautiful touch to the presentation. However, any sweet grape will do, so pick the one you like the most, preferably one that grows close to you.

≫ Kari makes an amazing ginger syrup (Morris Kitchen Ginger Syrup), which is what she traded for bread the first time we met. Obviously, you can also make this cocktail with your own ginger syrup!

CEVICHE

In collaboration with Elin S. Kann, **SERVES 6 AS A MAIN DISH OR 12 AS A STARTER**

I can spend hours at markets. But I do not really like to spend too much time in the kitchen. When I invite people for dinner, I do it mainly because I want a good reason to spend time with them. In my ideal dinner party scenario, I would cook before my friends arrive so we can chat while they try the wine. Or I would make something very simple, so dishes that take less than 30 minutes to prepare quickly become favorites of mine. If the recipe is easy to make regardless of how many guests are coming, then you have a star dish. This is ceviche.

With help from Elin's Peruvian family, we freestyled to make our own favorite.

To make the leche de tigre: Set a fine-mesh sieve over a medium bowl. In a blender, purée the lime juice, cream, chile, garlic, and the ice cubes until smooth. Add the onion; pulse three or four times. Strain the liquid. Season with salt. (The leche de tigre can be prepared 1 day in advance. Cover and chill.)

Using a steamer basket set over simmering water in a medium saucepan, steam the sweet potato until just fork-tender, about 30 minutes. Transfer the potato to a plate to cool, but keep the steaming water in the pot.

Steam the ear of corn in the same way, until crisp-tender, 2 to 3 minutes. Transfer to a plate; let cool completely.

Cut the sweet potato in half lengthwise and cut into ½-in/12-mm cubes. Cut the corn kernels from the cob. Reserve ⅓ cup/45 g kernels (save leftover kernels for another use). Cut the grapefruit sections into pieces ½ in/12 mm long.

Rub a large bowl with the cut sides of the chile; discard the chile. Put the white fish, salmon, two-thirds of the onion, half of the pomegranate seeds, and the leche de tigre in the bowl; stir well. Let marinate for 2 minutes, or longer if you like your fish "cooked" more. Fold in the sweet potato, grapefruit, and corn; season with salt.

Using a slotted spoon, divide the ceviche among small bowls or plates. Drizzle the ceviche with leche de tigre from the bowl; garnish with the remaining pomegranate seeds, remaining onion, and a generous sprinkling of cilantro before serving.

>> We added cream to the leche de tigre to lessen the sour and bitter notes in the ceviche. However, for a more classic style, you can just as well leave it out.

>> The leche de tigre that is left over from the ceviche is too good to throw away. Drink it as a shot the same night you serve the ceviche, or serve it to someone with a cold or hangover the next morning. Or shake it with a little bit of the grape brandy Pisco. It makes a great spicy cocktail!

>> Since ceviche is such a beautiful dish, I usually pour the leche de tigre into a nice glass carafe before I assemble the ceviche. It just makes the assembly a bit more fun.

>> If you are making the ceviche on board a boat or somewhere else warm, it is a good idea to add a couple of ice cubes to the fish as it cures in the liquid to keep it cold and prevent spoilage. But only add a couple cubes so you don't water down the final flavor.

LECHE DE TIGRE
(Tiger's Milk)

⅔ cup/165 ml fresh lime juice

⅓ cup/75 ml cream

½ habanero chile, halved lengthwise and seeded

1 garlic clove, smashed

4 ice cubes

½ red onion, thinly sliced

Kosher salt

1 sweet potato, peeled

1 ear corn, shucked

2 pink grapefruits, peeled and sectioned

½ habanero chile, halved lengthwise and seeded

12 oz/350 g white fish, such as fluke, flounder, or sole, cut into ½-in/12-mm cubes

12 oz/350 g salmon

1 red onion, quartered and thinly sliced

Seeds of 1 pomegranate

Kosher salt

Fresh cilantro leaves

THE PERFECT BURGER

Contributed by Linda Niklasson, **SERVES 4**

When we buy wine, we tend to consider the grape, aging, region, and other parameters. Beef works the same way—the feed, breed, fat content, and aging all impact flavor, texture, and appearance. For me, the ideal burger is tender and juicy on the inside and crispy on the outside.

Like an artisan sourdough loaf, a good burger patty has only three ingredients—ground meat, salt, and pepper—so using the highest-quality meat is critical. Meat from a well cared for animal always tastes better, and eases your mind and soul. Ask your local butcher for top-quality meat from a source that treats the animals humanely, and taste for yourself how the right meat makes all the difference!

2 lb/910 g ground beef

½ tsp salt

¼ tsp freshly ground pepper

FIXINGS

Hamburger buns, ketchup, mustard, mayo, lettuce, tomatoes, onions, pickles, etc. . . .

If grilling the burgers over charcoal, prepare the coals.

Gently mix the beef, salt, and pepper, taking care not to mash the mixture. Divide the meat into four portions and lightly form each into a patty. Each patty should be packed together just enough so that it holds its shape and does not fall apart.

Cook the hamburgers over high heat on the grill for 3 to 5 minutes on each side until the inside of the thickest patty registers 130°F/54°C on an instant-read thermometer.

Serve immediately with your choice of fixings.

>> In New York City, we used 75 percent chuck mixed with 25 percent sirloin because of the richness in flavor as well as the good balance of fat and meat. The final beef patty should have 15 to 20 percent fat to get a marbled texture and juiciness. The size of the grind makes a big difference in the tenderness of the burger, so, if possible, grind the beef yourself on a medium grind, or ask your butcher to do it for you. If the meat is processed too much, it will be too fine and you may destroy the fibers and end up with a tough patty. Packing the meat too tightly when you form the patties can also result in tough patties.

>> It is important to grill the burgers over a high temperature when you first put them on the grill, which creates a crisp outer surface that will trap the juices inside the patties.

>> Do not press the hamburgers with your spatula when they are on the grill, or you may squeeze out the meat juices into the coals.

>> To achieve a juicy burger, only flip the burgers once so that you don't disrupt the juices inside the patty.

MAPLE-ROASTED PUMPKIN SALAD

Contributed by Renee Baumann, **SERVES 6**

I traded a loaf of sourdough bread, baked in the NoMad kitchen, for this recipe. I asked Renee to help me create a vegetable dish to pair with a burger but that would steer clear of the more typical burger accompaniments. I wanted a veggie dish that would stand on its own, complement the flavor of the burger, and showcase the agricultural bounty of New York. Browsing through the seasonal produce at the Union Square Market, the idea came to her: kadu bouranee, an Afghan dish that she had recently fallen in love with. Traditionally, the sweet roasted pumpkin is served with hot lamb or beef and a cold garlicky yogurt sauce. She borrowed the flavor combination and then took some liberties, choosing simple culinary treatments, with just enough seasoning to highlight the ingredients.

To make the pumpkin: Preheat the oven to 425°F/220°C. Place the pumpkin cubes in a baking pan, drizzle with the maple syrup, and sprinkle with the coriander. Season with salt and pepper. Roast for 12 to 17 minutes, or until al dente.

To make the sauce: Cut the garlic cloves in half lengthwise. Remove any green shoots in the center. Finely mince the garlic. Stir the garlic into the yogurt in a medium bowl and let the flavors meld for 10 minutes. Season with salt and the vinegar, taste, and add more as desired. If you are using a tangy yogurt, you may not need any vinegar.

Toss the sunflower shoots with a little nut oil just before serving. Arrange a pile of shoots on top of the pumpkin and top with the yogurt sauce. Garnish with carrot slices.

Serve as a warm or cold salad, depending on your mood, season, or schedule.

MAPLE-ROASTED PUMPKIN

1¼ lb/570 g pumpkin, peeled and cut into cubes

¼ cup/60 ml maple syrup

¼ tsp ground coriander

Sea salt and freshly ground pepper

GARLIC-YOGURT SAUCE

2 medium garlic cloves

2 cups/480 ml tangy plain sheep- or goat-milk yogurt

Sea salt

1 tbsp red wine vinegar, plus more as needed (optional)

Sunflower shoots for garnishing

Toasted hazelnut or walnut oil for tossing

Purple carrots, thinly sliced, for garnishing

Midsommar

Midsommar Nights Magic, Anywhere

The Midsommar night is full of potency and hidden powers, especially when it comes to love and fertility. It is the night before the longest day of the year and the night that the sun never goes down. For many thousands of years, the Swedes have been using spells to please the higher powers and take advantage of the magic of this night. Back home, they say that if a woman is lucky, she will dream of her husband-to-be. This is, of course, something we all want to know, and so I have practically thrown myself into this tradition every time I have had the chance.

My older cousin and her friends taught the Midsommar tradition to me, long before I had any interest at all in boys. I think I must have been about age four when they first indoctrinated me. As we all know, one should start early. I remember the girls wearing long white summer dresses, or folk costumes, and their hair was decorated with braided wildflowers. They took me by the hand into the night to complete the long list of tasks that needed to be fulfilled. I was thrilled and excited, and walked through the night with my eyes wide open.

You can try this at home: Pick seven flowers from a meadow. They should each be a different kind of flower (grasses do not count). For every flower that you pick, you need to jump over a wooden fence or a hurdle. This is not too difficult to achieve if you are spending the night in the Swedish countryside. However, this is not always the case and so I have many times stretched the practice. There was the time in Paris when I gathered flowers from the middle of the traffic circles, and jumped every construction fence that Marais had to offer. Or in Colorado, in the United States, when my friend's mother ended up buying the flowers because we couldn't find enough growing naturally. After years of experience, I can now tell you what I've learned: You have to stick to the rules. Cheating does not work, whether you are in Sweden or anywhere else.

As with most important rituals, I recommend you first read the fine print before you start. There are two rules you must observe: First, you are not allowed to say a word during the whole process. And second, you are not allowed to laugh. These two rules have to be followed until you wake up the next morning.

There is also a way to make the spell a bit stronger: Pick the flowers from a churchyard in the night. I have not tried this yet, but it is a relief to know that there is a last possible boost if I ever get desperate.

When you have picked all of your flowers, you should go straight home. When you have finally made it to your bedroom, place the flowers under your pillow and fall asleep. If you did everything right you will dream about the love of your life.

So far, the Midsommar magic has not worked for me. I can honestly say that I have tried my best. It is painful, but I know what it means. Either I will never get married, or I am simply continuously doing something wrong. I like to think I know what I did wrong—it was all the laughing we did through the whole procedure. But if I'm not allowed to laugh, I don't want to get married anyway.

LAURA'S MAGIC MIDSOMMAR CAKE

Contributed by Laura Ximena Villanueva Guerra, **SERVES 12**

You have picked all the flowers, jumped the fences, and then slept dreamless like a stone. Upon awakening, somehow you were left with nothing more than a small bouquet of smashed-flat flowers under your pillow. No love met you in your dreams. You know that you must have done something that spoiled the spell, but you don't know what. Maybe you are even considering spending the next Midsommar night on your own. Don't do it. It's not worth it.

If you ever reach a point in your life where not even a Midsommar night session seems to help you find your love, don't panic—here is a back-up plan. My friend Laura Ximena Villanueva Guerra has created this Magic Cake based on my stories about Midsommar nights. It is a cake to share with the ones you love, or even better, with someone that you would like to spend the night with. Beware how much you eat—tonka beans have an aphrodisiac effect.

CAKE

6 eggs, separated, at room temperature

Scant 2 cups/240 g superfine sugar

1 vanilla bean

Scant 1½ cups/185 g organic unbleached all-purpose flour or type 405 flour

COMPOTE

1½ lb/680 g rhubarb, peeled and cut into ¾-in/ 2-cm pieces

1 cup/225 g superfine sugar

1 vanilla bean pod (reserved from the cake)

1 tsp grated lemon zest

WHITE CHOCOLATE GANACHE

1¼ lb/570 g Belgian white chocolate, chopped

1 cup/240 ml heavy cream

1 tonka bean

To make the cake: Preheat the oven to 350°F/190°C. Grease a 10-in/26-cm springform baking pan and line it with parchment paper. Bring a kettle of water almost to a boil.

In a small bowl, whisk the egg yolks and set aside. Using a stand mixer fitted with the whisk, beat the egg whites on high speed. Slowly add 6 Tbsp/90 ml of the near-boiling water and continue beating until stiff peaks form. Reduce the speed to medium and slowly add the superfine sugar. Split the vanilla bean, scrape the seeds into the egg white mixture, and reserve the scraped-out pod. (You will need it later for the compote.) Beat for at least 10 minutes, or until the mixture is glossy. Using a rubber spatula, gently fold the egg yolks into the egg whites. Sift the flour over the batter and gently fold in until smoothly mixed. Pour into the prepared pan.

Bake for 35 minutes, or until the cake has a light golden color. Let the cake cool completely in the pan.

To make the compote: Put the rhubarb in a large saucepan and stir in the superfine sugar. Add the scraped-out vanilla bean pod and lemon zest. Cook over medium heat until the rhubarb is soft, about 5 minutes. (Do not cook the rhubarb so long that it begins to fall apart and lose its texture.) Remove the pan from the heat and let the compote cool completely.

To make the ganache: Place the white chocolate in a medium bowl. In a small saucepan, bring the cream to nearly boiling over medium-high heat. Pour the hot cream over the white chocolate. Grate a pinch of the tonka bean over the top. Let the mixture sit, without stirring, for 5 to 8 minutes, until the white chocolate has melted. Then, slowly stir until the mixture is smooth.

Take the cake out of the pan and gently remove the parchment paper. Cut the cake horizontally into three thin layers. Set one layer of cake into the cake pan ring. Cover the layer completely with one-third of the ganache and refrigerate for 30 minutes. Pour half of the rhubarb compote over the set ganache and cover it with a second layer of cake. Cover completely with half of the remaining ganache and refrigerate for 30 minutes.

cont'd

CREAM FILLING

1 cup/240 ml heavy cream

2 Tbsp powdered sugar

3 sheets unflavored gelatin

2½ lb/1.2 kg strawberries, washed, hulled, halved, and leaves reserved for garnishing

MERINGUE

6 egg whites, at room temperature

¾ cup plus 2 Tbsp/200 g superfine sugar

1½ cups/210 g powdered sugar

TOPPING

1 cup/240 ml heavy cream

1 Tbsp powdered sugar

1 sheet unflavored gelatin

Edible flowers, such as nasturtiums, cosmos, hollyhocks, or violets, for decorating

To make the cream filling: Place the cream, powdered sugar, and gelatin in the bowl of a tabletop mixer. Let the gelatin dissolve completely, then whip until stiff peaks form.

Cover the ganache on the second layer of cake with half of the strawberries, placing them cut-side down. Cover the strawberries with the cream filling. Place the third layer of cake on top of the whipped cream. Cover the top layer with the remaining ganache and refrigerate for 30 minutes. Cover the top of the cake with the remaining rhubarb compote. Place the cake in the refrigerator overnight.

The next day, make the meringue: Preheat the oven to 250°F/120°C. Grease a 10-in/26-cm springform baking pan and line the bottom of the pan with parchment paper. Using a stand mixer, whip the egg whites on high speed until stiff peaks form, about 10 minutes. Slowly pour in the superfine sugar and beat for 5 minutes, or until the mixture is glossy and stiff peaks form. Sift the powdered sugar over the top and, using a rubber spatula, gently fold it into the mixture, folding just until it is incorporated and the mixture is smooth.

Spoon the meringue into the prepared baking pan, leaving a ¼-in/1-cm gap between the perimeter of the meringue and the inside of the pan because the meringue will rise while baking. Make peaks in the meringue by setting the back of the spoon on the surface and quickly lifting away, repeating until the whole surface has peaks. Lower the oven heat to 210°F/100°C. Set the pan in the oven and bake the meringue for about 45 minutes, checking every 15 minutes to make sure it is not browning. It should just dry, not color. If it begins to brown at all, lower the oven temperature by 25°F/5°C. When the meringue is firm to the touch, remove it from the oven and let cool completely.

To make the topping: Place the cream, powdered sugar, and gelatin in the bowl of a tabletop mixer. Let the gelatin dissolve completely, then whip until soft peaks form.

Remove the cake from the refrigerator, transfer it to a serving plate, and carefully remove the springform cake ring. Carefully peel the parchment paper off the round of meringue and set it on top of the cake. Cover the sides of the cake with the whipped topping. Decorate the cake with edible flowers or, like we did, with the strawberry leaves.

Slice and serve the cake. Store leftover cake, covered, in the refrigerator for up to 2 days.

>> There is a big difference between commonly sold granulated sugar and superfine sugar. The superfine sugar is essential for this recipe because it is easily incorporated into the cake batter and frosting.

>> The cake batter in this recipe is made without baking powder, relying instead on whipped egg whites to create fluffiness in the cake. Folding in the flour at the end of mixing the cake batter is also an important factor; adding the flour earlier would produce a denser cake.

>> The quality and the freshness of the eggs is essential. And the same goes for chocolate. Laura always used Belgian chocolate when we tested this recipe.

>> Tonka beans are banned for consumption in the United States by the Food and Drug Administration and there is no good substitute. If you cannot get tonka beans, use the seeds scraped out of one fresh vanilla bean instead.

MIDSOMMAR PÂTÉ WITH FISH AND LEMON

Contributed by Lotta Lundgren, **SERVES 6 TO 10**

Cooking for someone is an excellent way for your affection for them to take physical form. To cut the red onions so meticulously small that you still cry when you're done is practically the same as saying, "I love you." The recommendation to leave a relationship with someone who lacks the ability to express appreciation for your efforts is one of the best pieces of hands-on cooking advice I ever got.

5 eggs, separated, at room temperature

Grated zest and juice of 2 lemons, plus 1 lemon, cut into wedges

1¼ cups/300 ml heavy cream

1 tsp salt

½ cup/60 g cornstarch, sifted

2½ lb/1.2 kg white fish

6 Tbsp/90 g sour cream

½ red onion, minced

6 Tbsp/95 g caviar

2½ lb/1.2 kg new potatoes, boiled and cooled

Position a rack in the middle of the oven and preheat to 325°F/165°C.

Place the egg whites in a large bowl and whip until firm peaks form. Set aside.

In a large bowl, combine the lemon zest and juice with the egg yolks, cream, salt, and cornstarch and mix well.

Cut the white fish into ½-in/12-mm pieces and add to the egg yolk batter.

Stir the fish batter into the whipped egg whites.

Butter a 12-by-3-by-3¼-in/30.5-by-7.5-by-8-cm pâté pan or a small loaf pan and line with parchment paper. Spoon the fish mixture into the pan. Bake the pâté until set and firm to the touch when pressed gently with a fingertip, 40 to 50 minutes.

Serve warm, lukewarm, or cold with the sour cream, red onion, lemon wedges, and caviar. Since June is the time for new potatoes in Sweden, I serve the Midsommar paté with warm or cold cooked potatoes of the simplest kind.

The Bread Exchange

ROSE PEPPER GRAVLAX

Contributed by Carl Gustaf Elmlid, **SERVES 6 TO 10**

"Navigare necesse est," or "To sail is essential," is probably my father's favorite expression. It was written on every birthday card I ever got and mentioned at every graduation celebration or other milestone. My dad always left out the second part of the expression, "vivere non est necesse," which means "to live is not.")

I have thought of the expression "To sail is essential" during so many situations in life. Not because I am a big sailor like my father but because I think it helps me understand my surroundings wherever I am. It reminds me that it is easier to get myself from A to B if I take time to understand the waves and the wind. It is just the same with baking bread. I need to understand, feel, and go with the flow to get the dough where I want it to go.

Freeze the salmon for at least 2 days prior to making this dish. The fish can contain parasites, which are destroyed by freezing. Fully thaw and then begin the curing process.

In a small bowl, mix the salt, sugar, pink or rose pepper, and white pepper. (My dad's gravlax contains less sugar than many recipes. More sugar gives the finished gravlax a smoother texture and taste. But just like my dad, I like my gravlax with a stronger herb taste.)

Sprinkle two-thirds of the salt mixture on the fillet side of the fish. Add the dill. Place the second fillet on top, flesh-side to flesh-side, positioning the fillets so the thicker part of the bottom fillet is against the thinner part of the top fillet—"head to toe," as my dad says. Now place the fillets in a spacious freezer bag. Sprinkle the rest of the salt blend over the skin side of the fish. Close the bag and seal with another plastic bag to prevent leaking. Place the fillets flat on a large plate in the refrigerator. During the process of curing, turn the plastic bag four times so the top fillet becomes the bottom fillet and vice versa.

Thick fillets need 2 days to cure, while the thinner fillets are ready after 1½ days. Pour off the brine and scrape off the pepper and dill. Any remaining bone is now easy to remove. Cut the fish into thin slices on the diagonal with a long sharp knife.

When ready to serve, mince more fresh dill and cut the lime in half. Sprinkle the salmon with pink pepper and dill. Squeeze lime juice over and serve.

2½ lb/1.2 kg salmon fillet or 3½ lb/1.6 kg whole salmon, cleaned and filleted

5 Tbsp/55 g salt

2 to 3 Tbsp granulated sugar

1 tsp coarsely ground pink or rose pepper, plus more for serving

1 tsp coarsely ground white pepper

3 bunches fresh dill, plus more for serving

1 lime

>> My father often serves the salmon with mustard and bread as a starter or together with boiled potatoes as a main course.

Learning from the Master in Kabul, Afghanistan

Once upon a time, Afghanistan was the center of the world. And it still is,
if you ask the people of Afghanistan. Over the centuries, it has been a melting pot for many
cultures and traditions. It was at a crossroad on the ancient Silk Road connecting
Europe with the Far East, which brought rich influences into the Afghan culture.

Afghan dynasties, from the Kushans to the Ghaznavid sultans to the Durrani rulers, have all
contributed significantly to civilization. Uncountable wars have been fought on the soil
of Afghanistan and every invader has made a mark on the land.
And so it has always been, yesterday, today, and probably tomorrow.

Reading about Afghanistan today paints a picture of the end of their world as we know it. But what I saw when I went there to bake bread was not the end at all. I traveled to Kabul with my then-boyfriend, Matthias Gebauer. For him, Afghanistan is like a second home, but to me everything was new. Matthias works as a world correspondent for Germany's largest magazine, *Der Spiegel*. He has been traveling regularly to Kabul and throughout Afghanistan since 2003, writing about the war and its tight grip on the Afghan society from different angles. And naturally, when you have to cover war, the stories are filled with death and sadness. My experience in the region has been in Dubai, Egypt, and Doha. And none of these places were in the midst of war when I visited. Like many others, I follow the news of Afghanistan from a safe spot. I read about values that I have a difficult time fully understanding.

Even though I had never put my foot on Afghan ground, I felt as if I had already visited Afghanistan through Matthias's articles before I came. Much of that feeling arose from my fear for his safety there. I would check my phone for a message after reading about a suicide bomb that had gone off, and I could not fall asleep if my message had not been answered before I went to bed. Anyone with a loved one who is driving home on a snowy Christmas night knows what I am talking about. But this was my reality, and I sometimes had a hard time with it.

Matthias and I traveled a lot—about 170 days each year. Wherever we went, we wrote about what we've seen and what we find important. But our focus could not be more different. My stories are often painted in light colors, with the goal to inspire in a positive way. Unrealistic, some might say. War reporting is often painted in sad gray tones or in dramatic strong colors. Objectively I would call them realistic.

These reports from the war in Afghanistan are extremely important, but when I read them I do not feel like I am getting the full picture. As someone who has never been anywhere near war, reading these reports makes me feel as if war makes life stop. It is easy to forget that people were doing ordinary things—eating, baking bread, sleeping, laughing, making jokes, and falling in love—at that very moment when war touched them. War doesn't stop everyone from living; it just raises the stakes of daily life.

When Matthias returned to Berlin, or we talked on the phone from his Afghan cell phone, a number which was as common to me as his German number, I listened to his stories from a country full of hospitality, beautiful landscape, magic, ancient tales, loyalty, pride, and strength. It is a warmer and completely different story than what I read in the media. It is a story from the same world, but from entirely different perspectives.

One thing that Matthias seldom told me about are the women. Being male, and a Westerner, it is often hard for him to have contact with the women in Afghanistan. Especially without an Afghan man around. One thing he did tell me is that achieving peace in Afghanistan is dependent on giving women more power in that society. Many times my questions about daily life for Afghan women went unanswered. I often asked Matthias why he did not include the story he told me over dinner in the piece he posted for the magazine. Of course, he only writes about a small part of what he sees, but sometimes I feel as if the most interesting stories are left out. I want to read those left-out stories, the stories that make me connect with the people.

I was hesitant to make my trip to Afghanistan a chapter in this book. I was afraid that my motives would be misunderstood. Believe me, I do not feel the urge to travel to war zones. Rather the opposite. But, to not go to Kabul, when I was given the opportunity, felt wrong. I know I would have regretted it. And, on top of that, this trip was important for me and my life with Matthias. It has inspired me, just as every other place in this book has.

...

I believe we have the power—and the responsibility—to choose the way we see the world and our own lives. The view can be more or less positive. When the winter in Berlin seems too long, I try to enjoy a night with soup and a movie with friends instead of fretting that the spring is taking too long to come. Even in the most dreadful moments, we have the power to choose the shade of the glasses we wear. Most of the time, I choose the glasses with the beautiful and quirky lenses. Life just gets more fun that way. I want to see and acknowledge the imperfection. And to appreciate it. Within minutes after arriving in Kabul, my shoes were soaked in deep mud. I could have cursed the mud, but I decided to laugh and see it as an entry point to the whole experience. As if the mud on the streets wanted to initiate me into Kabul life.

This is my subjective way of making life more meaningful. Somtimes this approach works, and sometimes it doesn't, but I am the main loser if I do not manage to see it this way. I believe that trying to make the best of things is one of the most powerful ways we can make the world a better place. Enjoying time with friends, trying to make a little extra effort for others and to smile a bit more, has a way bigger impact on other people's lives than I usually realize in the very moment that it happens. But I do believe it is the way to go. Still, the world is full of larger imperfections that are painful to deal with. And to deny them is not a path I want to choose. It doesn't mean I believe that one has to run off to Afghanistan to tell a story. I really think that awareness and small local actions are enough. These simple inspirations are what I usually focus on when I write for my blog.

I find it difficult to write about my trip to Kabul and ignore the moments of fear I had, the sadness I saw, and the worried parents I listened to. I heard people tell me about slain relatives in the same manner I might say my mother has a cold. There was the time I was sitting in the car and was ordered to hand over my passport, after having been stopped by a screaming policeman carrying an AK-47 who was so high on opium that he didn't even notice the heavy rainfall. There were armed people everywhere and we passed armed check-points more often than one would pass a newsstand on the street in Paris.

We were given the vague warning "don't be in the wrong place at the wrong time" and then we found our-selves stuck in a traffic jam, right at a police checkpoint at eight-thirty in the morning, as I crossed my fingers that no one planned to detonate a suicide bomb that morning. I feared kidnappers before I came to Kabul, but then when I arrived I heard about all the Afghan women and children who are kidnapped every day. Ten thousand children were reported missing in 2012. I listened to a father who, since the son of a relative was abducted, does not dare let his five-year-old son play on the street in their quiet suburb, knowing what it means to his child and his wife to be cut off from the community life on the street.

But of all that I experienced in Kabul, the positive stories overshadow the dark ones. I believe that the warm stories about simple pleasures, which are just the same in Kabul as in Berlin or San Francisco, are just as important to talk about as the stories of war. These stories are what make us smile, and that makes a differ-ence in the world.

WOMEN CHECK

تلاشی زنانه

الله اکبر

۱۹۷

I arrived in Kabul together with spring. It was March 21 and the first day of the Persian New Year 1392, *Nowruz.* The first day of spring is an important holiday throughout the country and the Afghans like to go out for picnics and celebrate. This very day the soil was still wet from the earlier days' heavy rainfall, but the families did not seem bothered by that and the traffic jams to the parks and shrines were long. I was thankful for the wet ground that made the usually dusty and toxic Kabul air seem almost fresh.

The country was in a treacherous in-between position—there was no war, but also no real peace. To not get stuck in traffic, Matthias chose to walk to meet President Karzai in the palace, but for me, as a Western woman, I had to go by car everywhere. It did not matter that I covered my hair, and wrapped myself in my wool patu. The streets are just not safe. Not for me, and not for anyone else.

I came to Kabul to form my own picture of life there. My goal was to learn how to cook Afghan dishes. I wanted to spend time with the women. And I wanted to learn how they bake their amazing bread.

Visiting markets in Kabul was a new experience to me. I love to go to markets at places I visit, and learn new things by chatting with the vendors and shoppers. This morning I met only one woman vendor at the market—she was selling bracelets—and I bumped into just a handful of women shoppers, all of whom were wearing burqas. I learned that it is often the task of the husband in the family to buy the food, which would be terrible for me, because I love to spend hours at the market. If the women must go to the market, then they go in the evening. I was a woman in the market at the wrong time, but I love the morning sun.

I have never visited a country where bread played a larger role than it does in Afghanistan. The most common kind is the naan bread, with a taste similar to the Iranian lavash bread, or the Indian and Pakistani variants of naan. In Afghanistan, bread is just as much a part of the meal as it is a vehicle for other food, and so the Afghans use it instead of a fork and spoon, eating with their right hands only. The people I met told me they eat about one bread per person per meal. The flat breads weigh about 1 pound, or 455 grams, so that is a lot for one person. I love my bread with butter, but in Kabul I felt no need for butter. Instead, I ripped my bread into pieces and soaked it in salted goat milk yogurt from the ashak dumplings or used it to wipe the plate clean of the last oil and tomatoes from the burani.

In Kabul, bread is often produced in bakeries that are run by men. The price for a loaf is 10 Afghani, the equivalent of 18 cents in the United States. But there is another kind of bakery—the more traditional kind, called *nanwaee,* where the women bring their own dough, and the village baker bakes it in the tandoor for them. This is the most common kind of bakery in Afghanistan and these ovens are often run by women, who are responsible for the baking, and their husbands, who watch over the entrance to the bakeries. For me this was great, as I always have a hard time finding a bakery that will allow me to use their oven.

The women in town bring their bowls of dough and shape the loaves themselves when they get to the bakery. They leave the dough for its final rise in the bakery, which is warmed by the heat of the tandoor. Some go home and return a couple of hours later to pick up their baked bread. Some stay to chat and gossip with the other women in the bakery. One woman pulled up her sky-blue burqa, showing her face as the fabric fell down over her back like a beautiful bridal veil. There is a lot of laughter in the bakery. When I visited, we did not speak a common language, apart from smiling and laughing, but hand gestures and smiles are a form of communication that reaches over every border. We all shared the opinion that bread is necessary.

The bakery felt like a free zone. The wisdom of the other women there fell over me. Wisdom about men, and about what a good husband should be like. For the women who stay home most of the day, the bakery is the place where they go to spend time with women outside of their own families.

If a family can afford it, they will have their own tandoor at home. This makes sense for large families, but the women of these families miss the fun and the laughs of the bakery culture. The bread in Afghanistan is mostly baked in a tandoor, a deep hole in the ground, about 5 ft/1.5 m deep, with a wood fire on the bottom. The tandoor reaches temperatures much higher than a regular oven.

These tandoor fires are built with two kinds of wood. Archa, an oily wood that makes large flames that lick the walls of the tandoor, smells lovely, like juniper, and develops smoke that, together with the light that shines through the small windows in the bakery ceiling, creates dusty rays of light in the room. The tandoor is kept warm by heating it with balut or toot, slow-burning kinds of wood.

The dough they use is fairly soft, almost as soft as my classic sourdough dough. The baker flattens it out, similar to a pizza dough, and wets one side with water so it will stick to the wall of the oven. Sitting on her knees next to the burning hole, the baker bends forward into the heat and sticks the dough onto the hot inside wall of the tandoor. How she managed to lean into that burning hole over and over still amazes me.

The dough is left to be cooked by the flames and the heat of the tandoor wall for about ten minutes. To get the front side of the bread just as crisp as the bottom, the baker removes the bread from the wall with a long metal tong, and holds it in the low flames of the slow-burning balut wood. When the bread is done, one of the ladies in the bakery scrapes the bread residue clean from the oven walls, using a stick of archa wood or her hands. In the bakery, this became my duty, since they thought my way of dough folding was odd and only the bakery owner is allowed to use the tandoor.

I brought my own loaf to be baked at the nanwaee. Each time I did, the bread turned out amazing—airy, chewy, and crisp on the outside. When you bake it with sourdough, instead of the yeast that is often used in Afghanistan nowadays, the bread stays fresh until the day after it was baked. Before I went to Kabul, I had traded a loaf of bread for organic German flour since I did not know if it would be easy to get organic flour to feed my sourdough with. In Kabul, I mixed my flour with local wheat flour from the market to make the dough. I had to sift the flour because there were pieces of plastic bags and threads in it. Some days I used bottled water in the dough, and some days I used tap water. (Some families had their own private wells under their houses, providing them with fresh water.) I used Icelandic salt that I brought from Berlin, having traded for it with a woman earlier in the year.

With photographer Farzana Wahidy translating, I told the baker about the sourdough bread and why I did not use commercial yeast. She knew exactly what I was talking about. The other women in the bakery joined the discussion and we were loudly talking about the use of sourdough versus the use of commercial yeast. Back in the day, Afghan women had also used sourdough starters, which they started with a spoonful of yogurt, but nowadays many women choose the less time-consuming process and use commercial yeast. This enables them to have their baked bread the same day they make the dough (provided they started making it around six o'clock in the morning). However, they were totally aware of the advantages of sourdough. They told me that it is better for both the stomach and the heart to eat bread baked with a sourdough starter. That is more than many of my friends in the West know.

ASHAK (Afghan Leek Dumplings)

Contributed by Massuma Najafizada, **MAKES 48 DUMPLINGS**

My first Bread Exchange in Kabul was a loaf of walnut bread I baked in Shoib and Massuma Najafizada's gas oven in the outskirts of Kabul. Shoib had worked with Matthias for some years and had become a close friend of his, and soon became the same for me. His wife, Massuma, had invited me to their home to teach me how to cook Afghan food. I was going to learn to cook three of my favorite Afghan dishes. My sourdough starter was jet-lagged and so my bread could have made a better first impression, but Massuma's recipes turned out excellent. Wrapped in wool patus, the traditional wraps that Afghan men wear, we enjoyed the meal together on large pillows made out of Afghan carpets.

In Massuma's kitchen, we sat on our knees to prepare the ashak on an oilcloth on the floor. It was a practical way to work. Massuma's three children climbed all around us. The men waited in the living room, but out of curiosity they could not really stay away. Massuma was the center of attention.

LEEK FILLING

1 lb/455 g leeks, white and light green parts only, cleaned and chopped into ½-in/12-mm pieces

1 tsp salt

2 Tbsp vegetable oil

MEAT SAUCE

⅓ cup/75 ml vegetable oil

1 red onion, finely chopped

2 tomatoes, finely chopped

1 lb/455 g ground lamb or beef

One 15-oz/425-g can diced tomatoes

1 cup/240 ml water

Salt and freshly ground pepper

DOUGH

3½ cups/440 g organic unbleached all-purpose flour

2 tsp salt

10 Tbsp/150 ml water, plus more if needed

To make the leek filling: Drain the chopped leeks and transfer them to a clean, dry bowl. Add the salt and massage the leeks with your hands until they soften and collapse in size. The salt will soften them. Stir in the vegetable oil and set aside.

To make the meat sauce: Heat the vegetable oil in a stockpot over medium-high heat. Add the onion and cook, stirring, until the onion is softened. Add the chopped tomatoes and stir until heated through. Add the lamb and cook until browned. Stir in the canned tomatoes and water and bring to a boil over medium heat. Turn the heat to low and let the sauce simmer for 30 minutes to 1 hour, until it becomes thick and oily. Season with salt and pepper. (The oil can be spooned off if you prefer, but in Afghanistan they know to appreciate the fat.)

To make the dough: In a large bowl, whisk together the flour and salt and make a well in the center. Add the water to the well and mix into the flour with a spoon until the dough comes together. Divide the dough into twenty-four balls. Lightly flour your work surface. Roll out one of the balls of dough into a thin disk, about ¹⁄₁₆ in/2 mm thick. Square off the dough, cutting it into a 2-in/5-cm square. Prepare a small bowl of water to dip your fingers into for sealing the dumplings. Place a square of dough in your hand, dip the fingers of your other hand in the water, and wet the edges of the square. Place about 1 tsp of leek filling on the square in your hand. Encase the filling in the middle by folding over the top half, covering the leek. You should now have a simple rectangular dumpling that looks like ravioli. For a more constructed shape, gently fold the rectangle in half lengthwise and bring the two bottom corners together, pinching to secure and folding up the outer edges so the dumpling sits upright.

Make sure the dumpling is not wet and place it on a well-floured baking sheet. Continue making the dumplings until all the dough has been used. Do not stack the filled dumplings, as they easily stick together.

Prepare a plate, large enough for serving the dumplings, by covering it with about half of the yogurt sauce.

Bring a stockpot of salted water to a boil over high heat. Add the dumplings and boil for 10 minutes, making sure to carefully submerge the dumplings in the water with a slotted spoon from time to time. With the slotted spoon, very carefully transfer the dumplings to a colander and let them drain. When the dumplings are well drained, place them on top of the yogurt sauce on the plate.

Cover with the rest of the yogurt sauce and sprinkle the mint and red pepper flakes, if desired, over the top. (In Kabul we used dried mint.)

Top the dumplings with some of the meat sauce and serve, passing the rest of the meat sauce at the table.

2 recipes Garlic-Yogurt Sauce (page 145)

2 tsp dried or finely chopped fresh mint

1 tsp red pepper flakes (optional)

>> Without the meat sauce, the dumplings and yogurt sauce make a very nice vegetarian meal served with the Maple-Roasted Pumpkin Salad (page 145).

BOULANEE WITH DOOGH (Potato-and-Leek-Filled Pastries with Yogurt Drink)

Contributed by Massuma Najafizada, **MAKES 12 TO 15 PASTRIES**

Afghans say that the first day of each new year should be spent with loved ones. You should make this day the most enjoyable to ensure that the rest of your year will be the same. It's a nice alternative to the West, where many people spend the first day of the year feeling unwell after indulging the night before.

Massuma taught me to make these savory pastries, which are a New Year's Day favorite, but they are also enjoyed year-round. On hot days, the boulanee are served as a snack with doogh, a salty kefir-like yogurt drink flavored with cucumber and mint. Boulanee also make a great snack alongside any salad.

DOOGH

5 cups/1.2 L cold water

2 cups/480 ml live whole-milk plain natural yogurt

One 5-in/13-cm piece cucumber, peeled and finely chopped

2 Tbsp fresh mint, finely chopped, or 2 tsp dried mint

1½ tsp salt

BOULANEE

4 cups/500 g organic unbleached all-purpose flour, sifted

Salt

1 cup/240 ml water

1 lb/455 g leeks

1 Tbsp vegetable oil, plus more for deep-frying

1 lb/455 g baking potatoes, peeled

Freshly ground pepper

>> Some people make the boulanee with only leeks or only potatoes. However, I love how this recipe is a mix of both.

>> If an Afghan family serves boulanee as a main dish, they make four or five boulanee per person. When served together with a salad, one or two boulanee is a good portion.

To make the doogh: In a pitcher, stir together the water, yogurt, cucumber, mint, and salt. Refrigerate until ready to serve.

To make the boulanee: In a large bowl, whisk together the flour and 1 tsp salt and make a well in the center. Add the water to the well and mix into the flour with your hands until a stiff dough forms. Transfer the dough to a floured work surface and knead for about 10 minutes, or until the dough feels smooth, elastic, and has a shiny surface. Form the dough into a ball and set aside to rise under a cloth for at least 30 minutes.

Cut the leeks in half lengthwise, then chop the white and light green parts only, and place in a bowl of cold water to wash away the dirt. Change the water three times, or until you no longer see grit and dirt in the water. Drain the leeks and transfer them to a clean, dry bowl. Add 3 tsp salt and massage the leeks with your hands until they soften and collapse. Stir in the 1 Tbsp vegetable oil.

Fill a large stockpot halfway with water and bring to a boil over high heat. Add 1 tsp salt, then add the potatoes and cook until soft. Drain the potatoes, return them to the stockpot, and mash them finely. Add the leeks and season with salt and pepper.

On a well-floured work surface, divide the dough into 12 to 15 pieces. Roll the balls as thinly as possible into rounds about 6 in/15 cm in diameter. Prepare a small bowl of water to dip your fingers into for sealing the dumplings. Place a dough round in your hand, dip the fingers of your other hand in the water, and wet the edges of the circle. Spread 1½ to 2½ Tbsp of the potato-leek filling on half of the round. Encase the filling in the middle by folding over the top half to cover the filling. You should now have a dumpling that looks like a half-moon. Place the dumpling on a well-floured baking sheet. Repeat with the remaining dough and filling.

Fill a pot with vegetable oil to a depth of 4 in/10 cm and heat over medium-high heat to 365°F/185°C. Fry the boulanee, one or two at a time, in the hot oil, turning them as they cook until both sides are dark golden brown.

Serve with the doogh, instructing your guests to dip the pastries whole into their yogurt drink. Alternatively, you may cut the pastries into 2-in-/5-cm-wide slices.

BORANI BADENJAN (Eggplant and Tomatoes in Yogurt)
Contributed by Massuma Najafizada, **SERVES 6**

Afghanistan is the meeting place of four major cultural areas: Central Asia, the Middle East, the Indian subcontinent, and the Far East. You will notice it in the customs, and most of all in the country's food culture, which reflects the influence of so many different ethnic groups. This dish, also taught to me by Massuma Najafizada, is an example of that.

The dish got its name from the nickname of the princess who married Caliph of Baghdad in the ninth century. It is said to have been served at their wedding. It is an excellent side dish and makes a perfect companion to the ashak.

Fill a large sauté pan or skillet with vegetable oil to a depth of 1½ in/4 cm and heat over medium-high heat. Add 1 tsp salt. Working in batches, add the eggplant slices carefully to the pan, frying until golden brown and transferring the slices to a paper towel–lined baking sheet to drain. Repeat with the potato slices until all are fried.

Cut three of the tomatoes into ¼-in-/6-cm-thick slices.

In a deep 9 in-/23-cm cast-iron skillet, layer the eggplant, cover with the tomato slices, and top with the potatoes, seasoning each layer with a sprinkling of salt. Carefully pour the water around the perimeter of the skillet and set aside.

In another sauté pan or skillet, fry the onion over medium-high heat, stirring continuously until the onion has softened but not colored. Process the remaining three tomatoes in a food processor, or finely chop by hand. Add the processed tomatoes to the onion and cook over low heat for about 10 minutes. Add the canned tomatoes and turmeric, turn the heat to low, and cook for 5 minutes more. Pour the sauce over the layered vegetables in the cast-iron skillet, cover, and simmer over low heat for 30 minutes to 1 hour 40 minutes. The vegetables should be tender and beginning to lose their shape.

Cover a large serving plate with half of the yogurt sauce. Spoon the cooked vegetables onto the plate, trying to avoid getting much of the oil from the bottom of the skillet. If you like, garnish with chopped mint and dot with more sauce as decoration. Serve right away.

Vegetable oil for frying

Salt

5 eggplants, cut into ⅓-in-/8-mm-thick slices

2 baking potatoes, peeled and cut into ¼-in-/6-cm-thick slices

6 tomatoes

1 cup/240 ml water

1 red onion, finely chopped

One 28-oz/794-g can whole tomatoes, drained and sliced

2½ tsp turmeric

1 recipe Garlic-Yogurt Sauce (page 145), prepared without vinegar

Chopped fresh mint for garnishing (optional)

>> If you'd like to reduce the amount of oil, you can brush the eggplant slices with oil and grill or broil them instead of frying them.

Antwerp

Back to My Roots in Antwerp, Belgium

My family has been living in Sweden for hundreds of years. When my grandfather told me this, I immediately said, *"It cannot be healthy for a family to live and marry in the same area for too long. Grandpa, cultures have died out due to that."* But more than that, I thought that having such a homogeneous heritage was fairly boring. You can imagine my excitement when I learned years later that I actually have Belgian ancestors, dating back a few hundred years. I knew nothing about Belgium when I made this discovery. I imagined it to have poor weather, like other countries along the coast in Western Europe. I knew the country had been without a functional government for almost four years due to internal political conflict, which is difficult to imagine in a country situated in the snake pit of European politics. I remembered it being one of the last countries in Europe that had given up its colonies. In fact, the Congo was not even classified as a colony; it was the private property of the Belgian king. Consider that world view for a minute. My very limited knowledge about Belgium did not paint a very pretty picture.

For a European country, Belgium is young; its independence was not recognized before 1839. It is a clearly divided country with the Flemish-speaking north and the French-speaking Wallonian south. Despite the language differences of these Belgian regions, the Flemish and the Wallonians have one important thing in common: modesty. I can even say that I did not fully understand the meaning of modesty before I started traveling in Belgium. The Belgian people, please allow me to generalize a bit here, are less boisterous than their neighbors in France and the Netherlands. Someone described Belgium as a country of introverts who prefer to stay in the shadows. Compared to many European countries, you do not hear a lot about Belgium. But that is not necessarily a bad thing. When someone is not loud, it's much more likely that we will actually listen to them. I love the politeness I found in Belgium. Some might find it indirect, but it suits me perfectly. I never experience the culture there as arrogant or snobbish. Even when visiting the most exclusive places, I appreciate the warmth and curiosity I am met with. In fact, this is what I fell in love with first— the Belgian modesty.

And yet, Belgium has its contradictions. If you view Earth from the moon, Belgium is the first country you will be able to spot because throughout all of Belgium, every highway is lined with streetlights. Imagine that: a necklace of lights that you can see from space. When I realized that I have Belgian roots, I got curious about the Belgium-Sweden connection. Having Belgian, or rather former French Wallonian, roots is not uncommon in Sweden. In the seventeenth century, the Wallonians traveled north to help build the Swedish mining business. I know that it might be hard to understand how such a long-ago heritage would affect me today. However, knowing about my heritage awakened my curiosity and influenced me, a lot.

In 2007, I started to travel to the region for my work. Belgium has positioned itself on the European fashion map thanks to Antwerp. Still, Belgian designers have kept a low profile. Think Martin Margiela or Dries van Noten. No advertisements. No haute couture, only ready-to-wear fashion, but stunning just the same.

On my first trip to Belgium, Antwerp greeted me with a gray sky. The Schelde River did not bring color into the picture either. But as I walked through the antique stores of Kloosterstraat, I soon noticed that the gray shade there painted the perfect background tone to make me notice details. It is a special shade of gray you find in Belgium. Imagine the color of the fur of a Weimaraner dog. I call it Flemish gray. This gray has brown, earthy undertones. Close to taupe, but cooler. Just as the color gray in Zürich seems to be inspired by the bedrock, the Flemish gray seems to have emerged from the soil that is reflected in the gray sky. If I had to choose one favorite color in the whole spectrum, it would be Flemish gray.

What also struck me were the houses. I fell in love with the fact that they were not perfect and that the facades seemed to be allowed to show clear signs of aging. Everything felt real; there were no perfectly polished and well-maintained Disney-street views. Cracked facades and old flowerpots were everywhere. Most houses had a personal touch and none of them resembled their neighbors. Still, they had their perfectly chosen colors, which could, if you did not pay close attention, seem like no active choice at all. That is how natural everything seemed. When you went inside, you saw powdery, or rather dusty, shades of washed-out cream and warm grays and greens. And there were interiors with hard industrial influences combined with white, mustard, and black. There is a lot of black in this country. There were vases of fresh-cut flowers—and, just as often, dying flowers—with petals allowed to spread over the table. The well-styled homes I visited in this country were some of my favorites.

The gray lines in the city reflect the tangled history and current political strife. The contrast of a modest people and a contentious government situation makes Belgium especially interesting. Belgium is in many ways a divided country. Two major languages are spoken and there is no history of a joint cultural heritage. Still, there is one important thing that unites the people of Flanders and Wallonia: a love for good life. You see it in how they value excellent food and drink. Only France has more Michelin stars per capita. Combine that with modesty and lack of eagerness to impress, and you have the very comfortable atmosphere that I love. Minimal branding meets maximum style sense and supreme quality. That is Belgium to me.

BELGIAN WAFFLES FROM LIEGE
MAKES 12 TO 15 SMALL WAFFLES

There is one waffle that does not need any of the fluff (whipped cream, jam, powdered sugar, or even ice cream) that people put on lesser waffles. This waffle does not even need maple syrup. A bit of fresh fruit is always refreshing, but not necessary. The Liege waffle stands strong on its own. With sugar to caramelize its crust, this waffle is as good cold as it is warm.

1½ Tbsp light brown sugar

2 tsp active dry yeast

⅓ cup/75 ml lukewarm water

2 cups/300 g organic unbleached all-purpose flour

½ tsp salt

3 eggs

1 vanilla bean

1 cup/225 g unsalted butter, melted, plus 2 Tbsp for brushing

1 cup/200 g Belgian pearl sugar

In a small bowl, whisk the brown sugar and yeast into the water and let stand until foamy, about 5 minutes.

Using a stand mixer fitted with the paddle, mix the flour with the salt. Make a well in the center of the bowl and pour in the yeast mixture, then mix on medium speed until a shaggy dough forms, about 1 minute. Add the eggs, one at a time, mixing for 20 seconds after each. Split the vanilla bean, scrape the seeds and whisk the vanilla together with the 1 cup/225 g melted butter. With the mixer on medium-low speed, gradually mix in the vanilla-butter until smooth; the batter will be thick and very sticky.

Cover the mixer bowl with plastic wrap and let the batter rise in a warm place until doubled in size, about 1 hour 45 minutes.

Stir the pearl sugar into the risen batter. Cover again and let rest for 15 minutes.

Preheat a Belgian waffle iron and brush it with melted butter. Gently stir the batter to deflate. Using about 2 Tbsp batter for each, cook the waffles according to the manufacturer's directions until they are golden and crisp, brushing the waffle iron with melted butter before cooking each waffle. Serve hot.

>> Belgian pearl sugar is available at specialty shops and online. It adds a characteristic crunch to Liege waffles.

>> To make ahead, mix the batter but don't add the pearl sugar. Cover and let rise in the refrigerator overnight. The next day, let the batter come to room temperature, then stir in the pearl sugar and cook as directed.

>> In Belgium, a waffle is usually large enough to make me forget to eat lunch. Therefore, I usually make my Liege waffles half the size of what is common in Belgium.

CRÈME AUX NOISETTES ET CHOCOLAT (Hazelnut-Chocolate Spread)

Contributed by Sascha Rimkus and Petra Fiegle. **MAKES 1 CUP/270 G**

It's all about good ingredients. If you use hazelnuts, use the best hazelnuts you can find. The same goes for the chocolate and the sugar. The higher the quality of the chocolate, the better. There is a difference between regular brown sugar and light muscovado; you will definitely taste it.

It all started with a bread trade—one loaf for a seminar about German and Austrian white wines, led by Sascha Rimkus, part-owner of Berlin specialty food shop Goldhahn & Sampson. Sasha and I became friends, sharing the details of our experiences with Manitoba flour and mineral Riesling. Just as I am, he is crazy about good and honest ingredients. And he loves to tell a story. Goldhahn & Sampson is where I go to find inspiration through the ingredients. I think I have tried every variety of salt they sell by now.

½ cup/80 g hazelnuts (preferably Piemontese)

6 Tbsp/85 g butter

3 oz/85 g dark 70% cacao Belgian chocolate, finely chopped

3 egg yolks

Generous ⅔ cup/80 g powdered sugar

¾ cup plus 2 Tbsp/80 g hazelnut flour

¼ cup/60 ml crème fraîche

Pinch of sea salt

Preheat the oven to 350°F/180°C. Spread the hazelnuts in a baking pan and toast in the oven until they're aromatic, golden brown, and shiny, about 7 minutes. Transfer to a kitchen towel, wrap up, and set aside to cool. When cool, rub away the loose skins with the cloth, then finely chop the nuts, leaving some larger pieces.

Place the butter and chocolate in a medium-size heatproof bowl (such as a stainless-steel mixing bowl). Bring 1 in/2.5 cm of water to a simmer in a saucepan. Once the water is simmering, place the bowl on top of the saucepan to make a double boiler and melt the butter and chocolate. When fully melted, stir to mix and set aside to cool slightly.

In a medium bowl, whisk the egg yolks and powdered sugar until foamy, about 3 minutes. While whisking, carefully pour in the hazelnut flour. As soon as the flour is well mixed, add the butter-chocolate mixture. Using a rubber spatula, fold in the crème fraîche. Stir in the toasted hazelnuts. Sprinkle the salt over the top and stir in.

Transfer the spread to clean glass jars with lids and store in the refrigerator for up to 1 week.

SPECULOOS À TARTINER (Ginger Snap Spread)

Contributed by Sascha Rimkus and Petra Fiegle, **MAKES 2 CUPS/570 G**

When Sascha was living in Belgium, his idea of a perfect breakfast was good coffee, crisp baguettes, fresh and buttery pastry, and the ultimate breakfast heroes, Crème aux Noisettes et Chocolat *and* Speculoos à Tartiner *(a ginger snap–based spread).*

Sascha told me about a beautiful bakery with the lovely smell of freshly baked eggy brioches where he used to have breakfast. They had it all—the best crème de noisette and, even better, homemade speculoos spread. Even after leaving Belgium, he couldn't forget that taste. I am sure that Sascha and his girlfriend Petras's version does that Belgian bakery justice.

To make the cookies: In a small saucepan, bring the water and rock candy to a boil over medium-high heat, cooking until the candy is dissolved, to make 1¼ cups/300 ml rock candy syrup. Place the saucepan in the refrigerator to cool.

In a large bowl, mix the rock candy syrup, butter, brown sugar, cinnamon, and salt. Carefully add the flour and baking powder and knead well until a soft dough forms. Wrap the dough in plastic wrap and let it rest in the refrigerator for 2 hours.

Preheat the over to 325°F/165°C. Line a baking sheet with parchment paper. Unwrap the dough and form into a log. Cut the log into ¾-in-/2-cm-thick slices. Bake the cookies for 20 minutes or until set but not brown.

To make the speculoos: Set a small sauté pan or skillet over medium heat; add the cloves, white peppercorns, and cardamom seeds; and toast for 1 to 2 minutes, or until the spices are aromatic. Put them in a mortar and use a pestle to crush them into a powder. Add the cinnamon and ginger and grate in the nutmeg (about one-third of a nut). Stir to combine well.

To make the speculoos à tartiner: Put the cookies into the bowl of a food processor and grind into fine crumbs. Add the brown sugar and process to combine with the cookie crumbs. With the processor running, add the coconut milk, speculoos, and lemon juice. Keep processing until the mixture has a smooth, cream-like texture.

Ladle the mixture into clean jars, cover, and refrigerate for up to 1 week.

>> If you're short on time, you could easily use store-bought Belgian caramel cookies instead of making them from scratch.

CARAMEL COOKIES

¾ cup plus 2 Tbsp/210 ml water

1 cup/200 g brown sugar rock candy

¾ cup plus 2 Tbsp/200 g butter, at room temperature

½ cup/100 g packed light brown sugar or muscovado sugar

1 tsp ground cinnamon

½ tsp salt

3½ cups/440 g organic unbleached all-purpose flour

2 tsp baking powder

SPECULOOS

1 tsp whole cloves

1 tsp white peppercorns

1 tsp whole cardamom seeds

1½ tsp ground cinnamon

Pinch of ground ginger

Whole nutmeg for grating

SPECULOOS À TARTINER

8¾ oz/250 g caramel cookies (recipe above)

¼ cup/50 g packed light brown sugar or muscovado sugar

¼ cup/180 ml coconut milk

1 batch Speculoos (recipe above)

2 tsp fresh lemon juice

MUSSELS FOR MALIN

Contributed by Matthias Gebauer, **SERVES 2 AS A MAIN COURSE**

I could never speak for Matthias, so he explains how this recipe came into the Bread Exchange in his own words:

> *I inherited my love for traveling from my dad, who spared no effort to take me and our family to many seaside locations from the time my siblings and I were very young. Mussels with white wine sauce was one of the first things he ordered for us on those trips. Being a doctor, he explained over a glass of wine how this simple, inexpensive, and delicious meal contained all the good things from the sea in one dish. I had to rush to scoop up my share of the black shells from the communal plate before the rest of the family had eaten them all.*
>
> *This dish is so perfect because it has only a few ingredients, a short cooking time, and is the perfect partner for delicious white bread. Here I share a more experimental version, but it is as simple and delicious as the basic Belgian white wine recipe. This dish is prepared in two steps; first you make the rich broth and then you steam the mussels in it.*

2 Tbsp vegetable oil

1 head Thai garlic or other garlic

1 bunch green onions, white and green parts sliced

2 carrots, peeled and chopped

2 tsp chopped fresh ginger

3 stalks lemongrass, tender white part only, chopped

2 bay leaves

1 cup/240 ml dry white wine

1 cup/240 ml coconut milk

½ cup/120 ml heavy cream

2¼ lb/1 kg fresh mussels

Salt

Chopped fresh cilantro for garnishing

In a stockpot, heat the vegetable oil over low heat. Add the garlic and green onions and gently sauté, making sure not to brown them. Add the carrots, ginger, lemongrass, and bay leaves and increase the heat to high to pull the flavor out of the lemongrass, then add the wine and let it cook for a few minutes more. The longer you cook the veggies, the more flavor they develop and impart to the broth. Make sure to taste the mixture as it cooks, so you end up with the strength that suits your personal taste. To finish the broth, add the coconut milk and cream, adding more or less, depending how strong you like the taste of lemongrass and ginger. (The juices released by the mussels will add a nice sweet fish taste to the broth.)

Lower the heat to medium, add the mussels, and cover the pot to steam them. When all the mussels are open, they are ready. The steaming takes only a few minutes and you need to keep a careful eye on the mussels. You do not want to overcook them because they lose their tenderness fast. When the mussels have opened, divide them between two soup plates, discarding any that remain closed. Season with salt. Ladle the broth around the mussels, garnish with cilantro, and serve.

≫ When the broth tastes good to you, it's time to set the table because the mussels cook quickly and when they are ready, you will want to serve them right away.

≫ The amount of cream and coconut milk is a suggestion and can easily be increased or reduced to suit your own taste.

≫ We used a Sauvignon Blanc as a cooking wine for this dish. However, if you like more acidity, serve the dish with lime wedges on the side so your guests may adjust the acidity according to their taste.

≫ For a nice presentation, leave some lemongrass stalks among the mussels when you serve them.

Roadtripping in California, U.S.A.

We Europeans can be a bit cocky about our food heritage. We tend to think we have the best bread. I mean, we have France, right? And we like to think our wine is superior. Europe is the Old World after all. We like to point out that fast food was invented in the United States.

Still, I have my first visit to the United States to thank for my somewhat late development of appreciation for good food. I spent my senior year of high school in Dublin, Ohio, where I lived with the food-loving Davis family. My host mom, Nancy, explained to me the importance of time and patience in cooking; she would cook her tomato sauce all day. Her husband, Bill, taught me the do's and don'ts of shopping with a conscience at the supermarket. When we enjoyed their daily three-course dinners, all made from scratch, I learned that cooking is just another way of expressing love. And that the Europeans are not the only ones with a keen understanding of good food.

When I started working on this book, Berlin-based graphic designer Katrin Weber and I decided to drive up Highway 1 from Los Angeles to San Francisco and then to Sonoma County. We had never been over this ground before. There were no fixed plans apart from the goal to eat our way from one end of the route to the other. This proved to be easy.

As usual when I arrive somewhere via plane, the first task is to wake up the sourdough that has been slumbering in my suitcase. Six hours in the airplane cargo does have an effect. After arriving in L.A., the hunt for an oven began. I called up Gjelina restaurant in Venice Beach and they agreed to let me use their wood-fired oven. Inspired by the smoggy sunset that met me as my flight approached the City of Angels, I had prepared a pink-tinged dough, colored by beets. After trading bread with a photographer at Golden Bridge Yoga studio in Hollywood, Katrin and I started our road trip along the coast. Katrin was really keen to get in the water before we left Southern California, and the search for a surfboard trade began. In Malibu, we were lucky and traded my kale bread for an afternoon in the waves before we headed up north.

Trading my bread during traveling is one of the most thrilling, and exhausting, things I know. It demands a lot of time and flexibility. At the same time, it never ends up being boring. I always learn something new. The variety of people I get to meet is incredible and they always have a story to tell. I usually find them via my Bread Exchange network online. There is usually a follower who has interesting connections, tips for inspiring places, or a good idea on how to handle a tricky situation. I usually simply post where I am and within a couple of hours I have a date for a trade. The end result is always exciting and usually unexpected.

Guided by the barters, Katrin and I passed Big Sur and then San Francisco and started to make detours. We went to the wine region in Sonoma County and the oyster farms in Tomales Bay. The farm-to-table experience I had in Warsaw assumed a completely new meaning to me here in California. Fresh.

With the sourdough in the back of our car, we constantly had something to do. I have asked myself many times why people are so open to trading. Inviting us, two completely unknown Europeans, into their homes, sharing private stories, cooking for us, and sometimes offering us a night on the sofa. All in exchange for bread.

Traveling with a sourdough is like traveling with a small diva. You are completely tied to its mood and need for food, rest, and a stable temperature. When you think you are getting along great, it recedes and pouts and you have no idea what you could have done to upset it. *"I know we had a different plan, but I am just not in the mood right now,"* the sourdough seems to say. Or *"Today is just not a good day for me."*

I can't stand human divas, let alone sourdough ones. There were many times that I stopped, looked at what we were doing, and thought to myself, *"This is crazy. I'm traveling around with dough in my car, trading bread for anything. That is weird."* But in California it did not seem strange at all.

Thanks to the Bread Exchange network, I was connected with Spring Maxfield a couple of days after I arrived in the United States. Spring is an incredibly warmhearted woman who lives with her creative and full-of-life family in Santa Rosa, California. She is deeply connected to the food world there and invited me to participate in a secret farmers' black market in Sonoma County. Imagine an underground food market of goods produced in the most fertile of regions. Here, more than eight hundred farmers and food lovers exchange everything that is too good or special to get a fair market price for. It is not like the common farmers' market that we know from home, where everyone gathers at once. Instead this network offers its goods in private online networks and then meets face-to-face to complete the trade.

When the plums are ripe or the eggs are freshly laid, they are offered to anyone in the group for trade instead of sale. When the established markets fail, it is simply more satisfying to exchange their product with someone who understands its value in return for something they need. Why keep it underground? Well, it is just one way of protecting the group. Some barters are made in the gray zone of the U.S. Department of Agriculture's food regulations. Many of these items, such as unpasteurized cheese, are legal in Europe but not in the United States. There are cases where farmers have been sued for selling fresh, unpasteurized milk and have even lost their whole farm because of it. In the underground network, the trades are guarded by the like-minded.

The trip took unexpected paths, all guided by the traders who contacted me online daily, trying to get ahold of bread. In the wine country, we stopped in Healdsburg to borrow an oven at the Downtown Bakery & Creamery. I traded the bread I baked for six bottles of beer from Russian River Brewery. I baked a new loaf, flavored with beer and apricots, and traded it for fresh herbs from a garden outside Santa Rosa. We were offered beds and hotel nights. Pickled mushrooms. Salt. We exchanged bread for tips and connections to local restaurants and vineyards. We exchanged bread for family recipes. In Sonoma, Andrew and Adam Mariani from Scribe Winery invited me to bake in their wood-fired oven as the sun set, which developed into a pizza cookout with their friends. After some excellent wine, they offered us a night on the couch. In Petaluma, I borrowed a horse one afternoon. We traded for tomatoes that were such strange shapes they were unsellable. Their taste was so strong that I will never forget eating them with bread on the roadside over-looking the ocean on our way to San Francisco.

One night I got an offer to trade my rosemary sourdough for freshly made goat cheese. It was not just any kind of goat cheese, but unpasteurized goat cheese. And there is only one thing that I miss when I leave Europe—raw dairy. Raw milk, cheese, and butter are practically impossible to find in the States because production is restricted due to health regulations. If it weren't for the strict laws, you would undoubtedly find the best raw-milk butter in Vermont and the most complex raw-milk cheese in Point Reyes.

I think you can imagine my excitement when a trader offered to show us how to make this particular cheese ourselves. In fact, to trade my bread for the opportunity to learn something new, whatever it may be, is one of my favorite trades because I will have it with me forever. Katrin and I stayed for dinner and left late in the dark night. Backing the car out of the driveway, I didn't see the black pickup truck parked behind me. Crash. Katrin and I kept quiet and looked at each other.

We were in California and had just been trading illegal raw-milk cheese on the black market. We both knew this could mean double trouble. It felt absurd that something that is so good for you can result in a punishment comparable with one you get for carrying drugs or a weapon. We waited for ages for the police to arrive. In the meantime, we found the truck's owner, who served us homemade crumble pie while we waited. People are nice in California. The policeman came, excusing himself for being so late. There had been an altercation at a marijuana farm in the area. It was harvest season, which often causes such incidents, he explained. He was happy to be doing something else. Katrin and I smiled until our cheeks hurt and were truly happy when we got to leave the scene.

I know that it was good for my European biases to go on a road trip through California. I experienced firsthand what happens when you mix good soil, cool ocean breezes, and abundant sunshine. You get some of the best crops ever. Add a relaxed attitude about life. You get California.

SOURDOUGH PANCAKES

In collaboration with Karen Roth, **SERVES 4**

I was introduced to Karen Roth through the Bread Exchange network years ago. We never traded bread because Karen herself is a dedicated sourdough baker. In fact, Karen, a former Silicon Valley venture capitalist, does everything with the most powerful dedication. When I needed help in Los Angeles and posted a request, it was often Karen who connected me with an oven or offered much-needed advice.

Sourdough pancakes and waffles became popular in California during the Gold Rush when they were served to miners morning and night. Karen, her three sons, and I all share a love for pancakes. Especially that buttery part in the middle of the stack. Karen developed this recipe to achieve the fluffiness of a buttermilk pancake and the light tang of sourdough. I love the fact that you prepare it in the evening and then minimal work is required in the morning.

1 cup/200 g Wheat-Flour Sourdough Starter (page 45)

½ cup/80 g organic unbleached all-purpose flour

½ cup/120 ml buttermilk, at room temperature

2 Tbsp butter, melted and cooled

2 Tbsp brown sugar

½ tsp salt

2 eggs, lightly beaten

¼ tsp baking soda

The evening before you plan to serve the pancakes, combine the starter, flour, and buttermilk in a large mixing bowl. Add the butter, brown sugar, and salt and stir to combine but don't worry if there are still lumps in the dough. Cover with plastic wrap and let rest overnight at room temperature.

The next morning your sourdough mix should be bubbling and ready to cook with. Mix the eggs into the batter. It should have the consistency of thin mud. Now you can leave the batter to sit until you are ready to make breakfast.

Sprinkle the baking soda over the batter and carefully fold it in. Let the baking soda activate for 5 minutes, but not much longer or the pancakes will not rise properly. Heat a large nonstick sauté pan or skillet over medium heat. Add ladlefuls of batter to the pan and wait until the tops of the pancakes begin to bubble and the pancakes have risen to about ½ in/12 mm thick, then turn them and cook until both sides are golden brown. Repeat with the remaining batter and serve.

≫ Make sure that your starter is really energetic (expanding and bubbling), because a lazy sourdough won't be able to make fluffy pancakes.

≫ You can also use this recipe to make waffles. For a round waffle, use about ½ cup/120 ml of batter per waffle. Cook in a moderately hot waffle iron.

VEGAN BANANA BREAD

MAKES ONE 9-BY-5-IN/23-BY-13-CM LOAF

I am not a big fan of bananas, but I love this banana bread, inspired by Bread Exchange member Laura Ximena Villanueva Guerra. Personally, I think it tastes better every day after the day you baked it if you wrap it in plastic wrap and let it get nice and moist in the refrigerator.

Preheat the oven to 375°F/190°C. Oil or butter a loaf pan.

Sift together the flour, both sugars, spirulina, salt, and baking soda.

In a large bowl, mix the soymilk with the vinegar and let stand for about 2 minutes, or until the milk clots. Mash the bananas. Add the mashed bananas, olive oil, and maple syrup to the soymilk and mix until everything is well combined. Split the vanilla bean, scrape the seeds into the banana mixture, and stir to combine. Add the flour mixture and mix just until combined; do not overmix. Fold in the nuts (if using) and chocolate chips (if using). Transfer the mixture to the prepared loaf pan, smoothing the top.

Bake for 1 hour, or until a toothpick inserted in the center comes out clean. Place the pan on a cooling rack. When cool enough to handle, run a knife around the inside of the pan, invert the loaf onto the cooling rack, and set aside to cool completely before slicing and serving.

>> If you prefer, you can just as well use a nonvegan chocolate in the recipe.

1¾ cups/240 g organic unbleached all-purpose flour

½ cup/100 g raw cane sugar

⅓ cup/60 g raw brown sugar

1 Tbsp spirulina powder

¾ tsp sea salt

¾ tsp baking soda

½ cup/120 ml soymilk

2 tsp apple cider vinegar

4 large or 6 small very ripe bananas

¼ cup/60 ml olive oil

3 Tbsp maple syrup

1 vanilla bean

1 cup/115 g walnuts or pecans (optional)

Generous ½ cup/100 g vegan dark chocolate chips or pellets (optional)

SPINSTER SISTERS' KALE SALAD

Contributed by Liza Hinman, **SERVES 4**

After three days in the United States. I saw a common thread connecting every menu in every restaurant I visited. It was called kale. I had never heard of it at home.

I ate my way through the spectrum: kale salad (sometimes raw and sometimes "massaged" with salt to tenderize it), kale smoothies, kale chips, kale granola, kale soup, and kale brownies. And, of course, I baked my first kale bread. In Santa Rosa, I asked talented Liza Hinman from Spinster Sisters restaurant to teach me how to make her warm kale salad, which I served with my Beer and Dried Apricot bread.

2 slices white sourdough bread

6 Tbsp/90 ml olive oil

Sea salt

5 slices Delicata or butternut squash

1 shallot, finely diced

3 Tbsp red wine vinegar

1 Tbsp Dijon mustard

6 Tbsp/90 ml extra-virgin olive oil

Freshly ground pepper

5 oz/150 g Tuscan kale, torn into bite-size pieces

5 oz/150 g baby kale, torn into bite-size pieces

1 slice bacon, cooked and crumbled

½ Sierra Beauty or other crisp, tart apple, thinly sliced

1 Tbsp Roquefort cheese

Preheat the oven to 500°F/260°C. Make croutons by tearing the bread into pieces. (I like my croutons to be fairly large and so I break them into 1-by-1-in/2.5-by-2.5-cm pieces.) Place the bread in a bowl, sprinkle with 2 Tbsp of the olive oil, and toss with salt. Spread the pieces out over a baking sheet and toast in the oven for 3 to 4 minutes.

Toss the squash slices in 2 Tbsp olive oil to coat, sprinkle with salt, and place on a second baking sheet. Roast in the oven until the squash is tender when pierced with a fork, about 15 minutes.

In a medium bowl, make a dressing by combining the shallot and vinegar and let steep for about 10 minutes. Whisk in the mustard and then gradually add the extra-virgin olive oil while whisking. Season with salt and pepper.

In a large nonstick sauté pan or skillet, heat 1 Tbsp olive oil over medium heat. Turn the heat to low and add half of each kind of kale. Cook, tossing the kale until it is slightly warm but not wilted. Transfer the kale to a large bowl. Repeat with the remaining kale and 1 Tbsp olive oil.

Add the croutons, squash, crumbled bacon, apple, and Roquefort to the kale. Toss to mix. Add the dressing, toss to coat, and serve.

» Make sure not to use extra-virgin olive oil for the croutons because it tends to burn.

» If you cannot find baby kale, just stick to Tuscan kale or add your favorite kind of kale.

» I like to use Delicata squash because you can eat the skin, which you cannot do with butternut.

The Bread Exchange

CHÈVRE

Contributed by Spring Maxfield, **MAKES 2 TO 5 CHEESES**

Before I met Spring, I had never considered making my own goat cheese. But, like so many things, she makes cheesemaking easy (and delicious). This makes enough to share and, of course, goes nicely with lovely bread.

In a large stockpot, heat the goat milk over low heat to 86°F/30°C. Remove from the heat.

Sprinkle the culture over the top of the milk and stir in gently. Wait 3 minutes. In a small bowl, mix the calcium chloride with 1 Tbsp of the water and gently stir into the milk.

In another small bowl, mix the rennet with the remaining 1 Tbsp water, stir into the milk mixture, stir thoroughly, and cover. Let the mixture rest in a warm place for 12 hours.

Lay a good-quality cheesecloth in a colander set over a stockpot and pour the mixture through. The whey will drain, leaving you with the curd. Let the curd sit in the cheese-cloth, covered, to drain for another 12 hours at room temperature.

Form the cheese in the colander into patties and let sit at room temperature for another 12 to 24 hours. Sprinkle salt onto a plate or waxed paper. Roll the patties in the salt to cover the outside. Sprinkle dill onto the plate and roll the cheese to coat. Wrap the patties in waxed paper. Serve the cheese right away or store in the refrigerator for up to 2 weeks.

2 qt/2 L pasteurized goat milk

⅛ tsp mesophilic DVI MA culture (also called M4001)

⅛ tsp calcium chloride

2 Tbsp water

2 drops liquid rennet

Kosher or flaked salt

Dried dill or your favorite herbs or flower for decoration

>> Save the whey for another use. It is an excellent nutrition boost in bread and adds a dairy richness to the loaf. To use it, simply substitute whey for 50 percent of the water in My Simple Sourdough Bread recipe on page 50 and follow the rest of the instructions for making the bread.

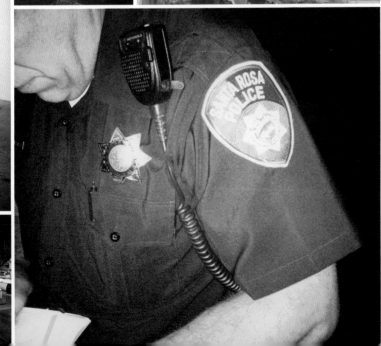

San Francisco

Home of the White Sourdough, San Francisco, California

When I was fourteen years old, I got the idea to move abroad. I knew that the smartest way to get my parents to allow this was to convince them I should study abroad. Of course, they thought I was far too young but I determinedly filled out the application, wrote all the letters, and practiced English by recording every episode of *My So-Called Life* on VHS, watching them over and over again. I collected photos for my personal portfolio so I would be prepared when the day came. Two years later, my parents finally agreed to let me go.

I decided my destination would be the United States. My dream was to live on the East Coast, preferably in New York City or Boston. The teenage me was fantasizing about preppy high schools and Ivy League style. I had a clear vision of what I'd find there: maple leaves, duffel coats, and tennis skirts. On my application I listed all the fitting activities: sailing, swimming, golf, and horseback riding. I constructed all the reasons I could conjure to ensure I wouldn't be placed in the kind of small town I already knew well from home. I claimed I was allergic to animals, and was a fan of the theater, concerts, and the opera. I only had one main stipulation—not San Francisco! I was terrified of earthquakes. I had the 1989 earthquake and Bay Bridge collapse playing in the back of my mind. It all went well in the end. I was sent off to the more stable state of Ohio, far from San Francisco.

Today, my childhood anxieties and fear of unstable ground have faded. And while madly researching bread for my Bread Exchange project, I learned that San Francisco is the home of the white sourdough. I knew that not even the threat of an earthquake would hold me back from going. When I got a call from a publishing house in San Francisco almost fifteen years later asking me to write down my Bread Exchange stories and recipes, it was not hard to convince me to get on a plane bound for earthquake country.

As Californians know, white sourdough bread became popular in Northern California during the Gold Rush in the mid-nineteenth century. While working their mining claims far from neighborhood bakeries, miners and gold prospectors nearly subsisted on naturally leavened (sourdough) bread and flapjacks, and so as a result the miners became known by the nickname "sourdough." Even 150 years later, San Francisco still claims ownership of the popularization of sourdough nationwide. In the 1950s, most of the country, as well as much of the world, turned to industrial bread making for its ease and increased profitability.

The classic characteristic of a San Francisco sourdough bread is its pronounced sourness, which differentiates it from the typical levain you find in France. The sour tang of San Francisco sourdough makes it an excellent match for seafood dishes, soups, and chowder—all favorites in the foggy Bay Area.

There seem to be a lot of myths about San Francisco sourdough. Some people even say that there is a certain strain of San Francisco sourdough bacteria that likes to grow only in Northern California. And that the starters that make their home in the Bay Area are the secret of successful bread. I have heard that if a bakery moves from one city to another, its sourdough bread will never be the same because the bacteria culture is naturally restricted to its location.

In the early '70s, a species of bacteria *Lactobacillus sanfranciscensis* was found in a sourdough starter that had been alive and propagated for more than one hundred years in San Francisco. But if you ask the scientists, this bacterium is not actually exclusive to San Francisco. It can be found in sourdoughs all over the world and is the predominant key bacterium in traditionally fermented sourdoughs. If you were to test my sourdough here in Berlin, you would probably find the same strain.

My sourdough bread has tasted the same regardless of where in the world I have baked it: New York City, Afghanistan, Stockholm, Antwerp, San Francisco. The variables have been whether I could find quality ingredients, the weather conditions, and my personal motivation and energy. In Gunnison, Colorado, the conditions were a bit tricky because I was not used to the high-altitude effects of baking at 7,703 ft/2,348 m above sea level, and at a humidity of 20 to 30 percent.

Apart from the philosophy of how a sourdough is supposed to taste, I believe that the magic of the San Francisco sourdough lies in its history. The idea that a sourdough has outlived its baker is captivating and can be just as powerful as its taste. It's the same with how the magic in my own sourdough starter is in the stories of people I trade with at places all around the world.

So why has sourdough bread always done so well in San Francisco? Is it the weather? The San Francisco weather is steady, never really too cold nor too hot. It's generally between 65 and 80°F/18 and 26°C, which is an ideal temperature. Cold is not life threatening for a sourdough starter, but heat is.

When I tried a slice of Tartine Bakery's bread for the first time—actually, there is no need to pretend to be civilized, as it was not a slice—I ate the bread directly out of the bag on my way back to the room I was renting. I had been searching around the world for the perfect sourdough loaf for more than five years. The bread that Chad Robertson bakes at Tartine is without a doubt one of the best breads I've ever eaten. The bread I ate out of the bag had that perfectly chewy crumb. Airy, but not dry. The crust was hard-baked, just like Bo Bech's bread that I tried years earlier in Copenhagen. Chad is a man with high ideals. I asked him if I could use his oven during my time in San Francisco. I told him about my motivations and what I was striving for. I told him about Bo Bech in Copenhagen, whose bakery had inspired me to eat bread again because it seemed to lack all compromise. I think that was what we connected over, the lack of compromise. Chad had just returned from Scandinavia, where he had gone for inspiration and had found it in the heirloom wheat and rye flours used in Sweden. Chad was striving for quality, which always carries a story. And I was striving for stories, without compromising on quality.

Somehow the journey of the Bread Exchange started in San Francisco without my even knowing it. It started with an aim I had, to make bread that I had imagined but couldn't find anyone making back at home in Berlin. It should be white with an airy, moist, and chewy crumb all at the same time. It would have a substantial dark crust as a nice contrast to the interior. And it would be sour and carry the distinct taste of grains. That this bread already existed, and had its roots in San Francisco, was unknown to me when I started baking in Berlin. I had never tasted Chad Robertson's bread; but still, his bread is as close at it gets to what I was dreaming of. And so this is where my journey ends; where it actually started. In San Francisco.

RUGBRØD (Tartine's Danish-Style Rye Bread)

Contributed by Chad Robertson, MAKES TWO 2¼-LB/1-KG PAN LOAVES

It was four-thirty in the afternoon and my German friend Katrin and I had just arrived in San Francisco. "Tartine is the best bakery I will have visited since Bo Bech's in Copenhagen," I told her as we walked down Guerrero Street.

"You will make me disappointed if you build it up so much," Katrin said, looking at me as if I were crazy as I bounded along excitedly in sync with Pilar, the bed-and-breakfast house dog, who had decided to join us for the walk. As we reached 18th Street, we came to a stop. In front of Tartine there was a long line of people waiting for bread that wouldn't come out of the ovens for half an hour. "I have not seen people queuing for bread since the '80s in the GDR," was all that Katrin could say.

The amounts for ingredients for this recipe are given only in weight by grams, which is how Chad Robertson ensures precision in the process.

310 g Rye Sourdough Starter (page 44)

180 g buttermilk, at room temperature

475 g water, at room temperature

135 g dark beer, at room temperature

20 g barley malt syrup

400 g whole spelt flour

100 g dark rye flour

15 g sea salt

525 g whole rye berries, soaked in water for 4 to 6 hours and then drained

135 g whole flaxseed, plus 70 g flaxseed, coarsely ground

105 g sesame seeds

45 g sunflower seeds

45 g pumpkin seeds

First, combine the starter, buttermilk, water, beer, and malt syrup in a mixing bowl. In a separate bowl, mix both flours. Add the flours to the water-starter mixture and mix by hand to combine. Let the dough rest, covered, for 30 minutes. Add the salt, soaked rye berries, whole and ground flaxseed, sesame seeds, sunflower seeds, and pumpkin seeds and mix by hand until incorporated.

Cover the bowl with a kitchen towel and let rise at warm room temperature (80 to 85°F/26 to 29°C) for 2 to 3 hours. Every 45 minutes, give the dough turns to strengthen it: Dip your hands in water and then gently lift the dough from the bottom and fold it over the top while turning the bowl 45 degrees; repeat three times until all four sides of the dough have been turned.

Butter or oil two 9-by-5-in/23-by-12.5-cm loaf pans. Dip your hands in water and scoop the dough into the prepared pans. Smooth the tops of the loaves with your wet hands. Let rise in the pans, uncovered, for another 2 hours at warm room temperature. Cover the pans with a kitchen towel and place in the refrigerator or another cool place (65°F/18°C) to rise overnight.

When you're ready to bake the next day, preheat the oven to 425°F/220°C. Score the tops of the loaves, brush with water, and bake for 1 hour 15 minutes to 1 hour 25 minutes, or until the internal temperature has reached 210°F/100°C or slightly higher. Let cool and sit for at least half a day or, better yet, until the next day before cutting. These loaves keep well for up to 1 week.

CRUSTLESS BREAKFAST QUICHE

Contributed by John and Joan Hull, **SERVES 8 TO 10**

I was going to San Francisco last-minute on no budget. I wrote an email to John and Joan Hull, who I had heard run an amazing bed-and-breakfast on lower Haight Street. I explained the Bread Exchange project and that I needed to come to town to meet the publisher for my book. "Sorry, we are fully booked," Joan answered. "But I do have a small bed in the laundry room that you can have. Free of charge." So I went.

It was the perfect match. I was jet-lagged and hanging out writing in the kitchen from four-thirty on every morning. Their black curly-haired dog, Pilar, joined me, and just an hour later Joan and John woke up to cook breakfast for their guests; I got to try everything hot off the stove. John baked with a forty-year-old sourdough, using a starter he had inherited from his father. We talked about world travels and shared inspiration. They showed me their San Francisco. They told me about the Summer of Love in the Haight and how it had been for them to leave New York City behind back then. We talked life. And looking at them, I thought, "This is what love looks like."

The evening before you plan to serve the quiche, butter a 9-in/23-cm pie plate. Whisk the eggs with the flour and baking powder. Add the grated cheese and cottage cheese and stir it all together into a batter. Add the chiles and butter and stir to mix well. Pour the batter into the pie plate. Cover with plastic wrap and let the quiche chill in the refrigerator overnight.

The next morning, let the quiche come to room temperature for 30 minutes. Preheat the oven to 350°F/180°C. Bake for 40 minutes, or until the mixture is set in the middle when you jiggle the pie plate. Remove from the oven and let cool for at least 10 minutes before cutting and serving.

5 eggs

¼ cup/30 g organic unbleached all-purpose flour

½ tsp baking powder

1 cup/115 g grated cheese

1 cup/225 g low-fat cottage cheese

One 4-oz/113-g can roasted mild chiles or 1 tsp mild chile powder

⅓ cup/75 g butter, melted

>> Select your cheese depending on how strong you like your cheese in the morning. I usually make the quiche with a fairly mature cheese like aged Gouda or Gruyère.

CAPONATA

Contributed by Jakob Padberg, **MAKES 6½ LB/3 KG**

All the ingredients you need for this dish seem like a giant effort, but in the end, it is well worth it.
Make loads of it, as it gets even better after a couple of days in the refrigerator, and serve it as antipasto,
with pasta, or as a side with a dry-aged bistecca fiorentina. This recipe will make a large batch, ideal
for guests, but you can easily divide it in half.

Place the eggplants in a colander set in a bowl, sprinkle with salt, and let drain for at least 2 hours. After 2 hours, blot the eggplants dry with paper towels.

Fill a deep fryer or Dutch oven with vegetable oil to a depth of 2 in/5 cm and heat over medium-high heat to 350°F/180°C. Line a large baking sheet with several layers of paper towels. Add the celery to the hot oil and fry until it is soft and golden brown. Using a slotted skimmer, transfer the celery to the baking sheet and sprinkle with some of the oregano. When the oil has returned to 350°F/180°C, fry the eggplants, fennel (if using), and zucchini (if using) in the same way, one at a time, transferring each to the baking sheet and sprinkling with oregano.

Heat fresh vegetable oil in a separate sauté pan or skillet over medium heat. Sauté the onion, garlic, and parsley stems until the onion is beginning to brown. Transfer to a separate plate lined with paper towels and season with salt and pepper. Add the diluted tomato purée and sugar to the pan and cook until the water has mostly evaporated and the sugar is caramelizing. Stir in the vinegar.

Add the tomatoes and cook for about 10 minutes. Add the olives, raisins, capers (if using), and chocolate. Cook until the sauce has thickened and is the consistency of mash rather than sauce. Transfer to a serving bowl and stir in the fried vegetables. Add the basil and season with salt, pepper, and a dash more vinegar, as desired. Drizzle with extra-virgin olive oil and cover with plastic wrap. Let cool at room temperature for at least 2 hours. Through the gentle cooling, the different flavors will blend into something remarkable.

Before serving, sprinkle the chopped parsley leaves, almonds, and pine nuts over the top of the caponata.

>> Try to use nice firm eggplants with very few seeds.

>> Don't cut the eggplants too small or they will absorb too much oil.

6 eggplants, cut into 1-in/2-cm chunks

Salt

Vegetable oil for deep-frying

3 celery stalks, coarsely chopped

Fresh oregano, minced, for sprinkling

½ bulb fennel, cut into ⅓-in-/ 8-mm-thick slices (optional)

1 zucchini, cut into ½-in-/ 1-cm-thick slices (optional)

1 red onion, finely chopped

3 garlic cloves

2 parsley stalks, leaves and stems separated and chopped

Freshly ground pepper

2 Tbsp tomato purée, thinned with 1 tsp water

1 Tbsp granulated sugar

5 Tbsp/75 ml red wine vinegar, plus more if needed

1 cup/250 g canned crushed tomatoes

¾ cup/150 g pitted green olives, coarsely chopped

½ cup/85 g golden raisins

¼ cup/40 g capers, rinsed and drained (optional)

2 Tbsp finely chopped unsweetened chocolate

2 large bunches fresh basil, torn or coarsely shredded

Extra-virgin olive oil for drizzling

1 cup/120 g blanched almonds, toasted and coarsely chopped

⅓ cup/50 g pine nuts, lightly toasted

CONTRIBUTOR CREDITS

Many people have helped me create this book. No payment has been exchanged for the illustrations, design, contributors' recipes, recipe testing, and many of the photographs. I have traded only my bread for the contributors' time, expertise, and work. In addition to these contributors, so many friends joined for the events in this book and others wrote or tested the recipes featured in every chapter. And so many people have let me borrow their ovens. I could not have done this book without you. Specifically, I would like to acknowledge the following:

For the Berlin chapter, I would like to thank Mirjam Wählen for photography at the dinner. I would like to thank Karen, Anton, and Christian Boros for opening their home for the Bread Exchange. A great thank-you to everyone from the Bread Exchange who came to the event. Thanks to Lara Maria Gräfen, who traded wine for bread, offered good ideas, and helped me prepare for the various photo shoots, especially the Berlin event. I am very thankful for the support of two of my favorite German vineyards, Meier Näkel and Weiser Künstler, as well as for Berlin chocolate manufacturer Bon Voudo. Thanks to the Swedish embassy in Berlin. Thank you to Oliver Kann for making music. To Lisa Frischemeier, who helped correct the German text. Thanks to Julia Breton, Cynthia Barcomi, Laura Ximena Villanueva Guerra, Petra Fiegle from deli-cat, Sarah Sheikh, Anna Küfner, Conrad Fritzsch, and John Benjamin Savary. And to Chris Kippenberger for making the movie at the bunker and to Anne Clark and Trickski for sharing their music.

For the Stockholm chapter, I would like to thank photographer Fredrik Skogkvist for documenting the crayfish party. I also want to thank Anne Larsson, Katharina Cederholm, Henrik Jessen, Devi Brunson, Mathin Lundgren, Mathias Dahlgren, Per Styregård, and Martin Bundock for their support locally. To Sandra Löfgren and Alex Poltrago, thanks for helping with all the preparations for the photoshoot and for the transportation with your lovely wooden boat. Big thank-you to Dennis Persson and the team behind HOPE-Sthlm. Visit Sweden has been a great help throughout the whole book production. Thanks to Absolut Vodka, for your support. Thanks also to Alexander Kovacevic, Alf Tumble, and Pär Lernström. And a big thank-you to the staff of the full-rigged ship *af Chapman* where the crayfish dinner was shot.

For the Bavaria chapter, I would like to thank photographer Yorick Carroux for capturing the brunch. I would like to thank Amely Steckert and Christine Schmitt from Rösler Haus, Nicky Stich, Stefanie Doll, Inger Elmlid Nolfelt, and Sasha Gora. Thanks to the beautiful Stählemüle for supporting with schnaps. Also thanks to Güde Messer for support with the German handcrafted bread knives. A great thank-you to Ingrid Doll for sending a large care package of meat for our brunch. Also, thanks to Nigel Cabourn and Peak Performance for making great winter clothing.

For the Warsaw chapter, I want to thank Maria Zaleska and Tymek Jezierski for connecting me so well in Warsaw. Jakub Jezierski and Magdalena Ponagajbo, thank you for sharing all your thoughts about Polish food heritage with me. Robert Serek for showing me his Warsaw. Thanks, too, to Dorota Żylewicz for supporting me with Vestal vodka. And to Anne Applebaum, for her great take on Polish food.

For the New York City chapter, I would like to thank Ira Chernova for photography. I would like to thank Agency V for connecting me with the beautiful wines from Friends of Truths. A special thank-you to Kathrin Prädikow for giving my sourdough a future home in NYC. Thanks to James Widegren, Katharina Riess, Kari Morris, Taylor Patterson, Deirdre Malone, Nhung Nguyen, Kate Cunningham, Nicole Salazar, Nancy Bachmann, Vilislava Petrova, Renee Baumann, and Linda Niklasson for all their help in New York City. And to Linda Ehrl, Elin S. Kann, Mel Barlow, and Annabelle Dunne, thank you for getting good people together even though you could not be there yourself. Sylvia Kann and Fabian Johow for your inputs on how to make ceviche. Thanks to the team behind the Swedish cafe Fika who did everything to find me a suitable oven. Thanks to Karin Hesselvik, and Converse, for your support. Thanks to Nicki and Russ & Daughters for connections and support during the preparation—your shop is an inspiration. Thanks to Daniel Humm and Mark Welker from NoMad for letting me borrow your oven. And to Gina Hamadey from *Food & Wine* magazine for letting me use your rooftop.

For the Midsommar chapter, I would like to thank photographer Antje Taiga Jandrig for capturing the ladies' picnic. Thanks also to the Blumenladen in Marienburgerstrasse. I appreciate my cousin, Tina Cifrulak (Bråmå), for inspiring me. Big thank-yous go to Saskia Ries, Laura Ximena Villanueva Guerra, Theresa Leuschner, Ellie Kulas, Lotta Lundgren, and Carl-Gustaf Elmlid.

The Kabul chapter would never have been possible if it were not for Matthias Gebauer and Shoib Najafiz-ada from the German magazine *Der Spiegel*. Their support and connections have been priceless. Massuma, Basher, and, again, Shoib, you made me feel so welcome! Thank you to Joel van Hoedt for trading the beautiful introductory image that opens this chapter in exchange for a jar of Sascha Rimkus's Belgian chocolate spread, salted French butter, and a loaf of my bread. I would also like to thank photographer Farzana Wahidy for her beautiful and important work portraying Afghan women and for helping me translate in the bakery. Thanks to the nanwaee for letting me join in their baking. Also thanks to Claudia Nassif as well as Maryam Montague from My Marrakech. Thanks to Mr. Kahn and Mr. Bauer at Serena Hotel in Kabul. Thank you Faridulhaq Durani and designer Rahim Walizada from Design Cafe for great inputs and amazing food. Also thanks to Haje Mujeb from beautiful interiors store Nomad, who helped out with connections and knowledge on ancient Afghan handcraft, and to John Wendle and Lydia Sparrow for helping out more than once. Thanks to Gahl Burt and Anja Niedringhaus for helping me with connections. The talented craftsmen at Turquoise Mountain carved the most beautiful baking shovel that I could ever have dreamed of.

For the Antwerp chapter, I would like to thank Visit Flanders for their support. Also a large thank-you goes to the beautiful hotel Boulevard Leopold in Antwerp, where I shot the mussels dinner, as well as to the hotel Chambre en Ville in Brussels. A great big thank-you to Debbie Pappyn and David De Vleeschauwer, founders of the beautiful travel site www.classetouriste.be, for sharing the Antwerp image with me. And, again, thanks to Sascha Rimkus and Petra Fliege, who out of a shared fascination with Belgian food, shared their recipes with me.

For the California chapter, I would like to thank Eric Anderson, who after only bumping in to me at his New York restaurant, Calliope, gave us a home in Santa Rosa and connected me with the great Spring Maxfield. Also thanks to Andrew and Adam Mariani from Scribe winery for letting us crash on their sofa after a late-night baking session and great wine. Gratitude goes to Gjelina in Venice Beach, Russian River Brewing Company, Spinster's Sisters in Santa Rosa, Downtown Bakery & Creamery in Healdsburg, and Dave from Levi's XX for letting me borrow ovens at the last minute. Thanks to Spring Maxfield and Nancy Bachmann for inviting me to stay with you. You made this trip even richer. Thanks to Karen Roth for helping out with connections in California, and everywhere else where I have been in the world. And a huge thank-you to the farmers' black market for all the help, trades, and exciting connections!

For the San Francisco chapter, I would like to thank Joan and John from the Parsonage, for taking me under your wings; Jen Murphy from *Afar* magazine for letting me stay at your home and giving me the best California connections possible; David Noel and Soundcloud for your support; Luke Abiol for images, and thanks to Chad and his team at Tartine Bakery for letting me use your oven. Also thanks to Randall E. Kay for your support and genuine interest in my project.

Fred Bschaden, photographer

Ira Chernova, photographer

Laura Ximena Villanueva Guerra, recipe creator

Martin Bundock, recipe creator

Antje Taiga Jandrig, photographer

Maria Zaleska, indispensable helper

Ann Larsson, indispensable helper

Rahel Morgen & Jakob Padberg, recipe creators

Matthias Gebauer, recipe creator and indispensable helper

Joel van Houdt, photographer

Christine Schmitt, recipe creator

Anna Küfner, recipe creator

Kheira Linder, illustrator

Elin S. Kann, recipe creator

Conrad Fritzsch, recipe creator, inspiration, and indispensable helper

Sasha Gora, recipe creator and indispensable helper

Lotta Lundgren, recipe creator

Lara Maria Gräfen, indispensable helper

Liza Hinman, recipe creator

Katherine Sacks, indispensable helper

Sascha Rimkus & Petra Fiegle, recipe creators

John & Joan Hull, recipe creators and inspirations

Yorick Carroux, photographer

Anne Applebaum, recipe creator

Mirjam Wählen, photographer

Nicole Salazar, recipe creator

Massuma Najafizada, recipe creator

Renee Baumann, recipe creator

Kerstin Pistorius, indispensable helper

Nicole Stich, recipe creator

Luke Abiol, photographer

Fredrik Skogkvist, photographer

Mathin Lundgren, recipe creator

John Benjamin Savary, recipe creator and indispensable helper

Katrin Weber, designer

Karen Roth, recipe creator

Gisela Williams, writer

Jakub Jezierski, recipe creator

Mathias Dahlgren, recipe creator

Shantanu Starick, photographer

Kari Morris, recipe creator

Spring Maxfield, recipe creator

The Elmlids, recipe creators and supporters

Stefanie & Ingrid Doll, recipe creators

Chad Robertson, recipe creator

Karen Boros, recipe creator

Robert Serek, recipe creator

Linda Niklasson, recipe creator

David De Vleeschauwer, photographer

ACKNOWLEDGMENTS

To the Bread Exchange community: Every trade you prepared, every meeting we had has made me believe in the meaningfulness of this project. The existence of the Bread Exchange has been totally dependent on the curiosity and goodwill of the people who take part in the trading, sharing, spreading, and supporting. Above all, I would like to thank everyone who has traded with me in the Bread Exchange project. You know who you are. Thank you again.

I would like to thank my family, Inger, Carl-Gustaf, and Eric Elmlid, for their love and support and also for their critical thinking, which has made me even more determined to continue on whatever path I have decided to take in life. I have them to thank for my curiosity, too.

To Katrin Weber, who, in exchange for endless loaves of bread and road tripping through California, did a great job on the layout of the book.

To Gisela Williams, for endless inspiration and good spirit.

To Kerstin Pistorius and Katherine Sacks, for reading everything and leading me in the right direction in the most motivating way possible.

Thanks to Matthias Gebauer, for kicking me in certain directions and for being a great travel companion and supporter. And for his patience.

To Sasha Gora, Alexander Matt, Gisela Williams, Adeline Thomas, Saskia Ries, and Alexander Pache, for reading, always being there, and giving great input.

To photographer Mirjam Wählen for her images and for all good times throughout the process of this book.

To illustrator Kheira Linder for her beautiful map of the Bread Exchange journey.

Thanks to everyone who replied to my blog posts and helped with testing recipes.

Thanks also to everyone out there who connected me with good people. Only good things can come to all when we share our networks with others.

To my dear friends Alexander Pache, Adeline Thomas, Martin Bundock, Linda Niklasson, Philipp Solf, Paul Hug, John Benjamin Savary, Lara Maria Gräfen, James Widegren, and Conrad Fritzsch for your fascination with the Bread Exchange, which has truly been motivational.

To Bo Bech, for getting me back to eating bread and creating the loaf to which I have compared every loaf I have tasted ever since.

To Chad Robertson from Tartine Bakery, who makes one of the best breads I have ever had.

To Manfred Enockson and Lars Gustavsson, for taking me under your wings and teaching me when I started as a freshman baker.

To Martin Johansson, who runs the Swedish bread blog Pain de Martin.

Thanks to everyone who patiently ate my often not-so-good bread in the beginning and gave critiques so I could get better. Especially to my neighbor, Herr Nofftz.

To the teams behind Levi's XX, Manufactum, and Alstermo Bruk. The way you are preserving and honoring history is inspiring.

Thank you Konradin Resa, for making that first trade of concert tickets. And thank you Nanna Beyer, for being the link to Konradin! And to Elias Redstone, who in 2008 triggered the idea of turning my bread sharing into bread trading.

Thank you to everyone at Freunde von Freunden for your endless support. Great thank you to the sweet team behind BOLD PR in Berlin/L.A. as well as the food loving PR Agency A.W.B. in Stockholm for supporting my project. Thanks to Nicolas Bregenzer and Jakob Padberg from We Are Blessed for helping out when my website crashed in the middle of the night. And thanks to Design Hotels for supporting my journey in exchange for bread.

To Lotta Lundgren, who has inspired me so much—as a person, a woman, and a food lover.

A big thank-you to everyone at Chronicle Books in San Francisco: Publisher Christine Carswell; my editor, Lorena Jones; Designer Vanessa Dina; Managing Editor Doug Ogan; Copyeditor Cheryl Redmond; Production Manager Steve Kim; Editors Sarah Billingsley, Amy Treadwell, and Elizabeth Yarborough; Publicist David Hawk; Marketing Manager Peter Perez; Rights Director Johan Almqvist; and, of course, the entire sales team.

Finally, a big personal thank-you to Alexander Matt, Daniela Müller Brunke and Jens Pieper, Nanna Beyer, Hanna and Kristian Sanden Sydnes, Emma and Anders Röpke, Fee Kyriakopolous, Kai Bergmann, Daniel Becker, Andreas Berschauer, Emma Jessen Krut, Saskia Ries, Lara Maria Gräfen, Sasha Gora, Ellie Kulas, Anne Larsson, Elin S. Kann, Rahel Morgen, Billi Offergeld, Luke Abiol, Shantanu Starick, Ricky Alston, Eva Maria Golan and Wolfgang Ae, Gabriella Lundgren, Anna Küfner, Anders Nordström, Teena Denzinger, Stefanie Walter, Jessica Klimach, Rahel Morgen, Emilie Bruner, Stephanie Bothor, Ailine Liefeld, Jade Lai, Svenja Evers, Sarah Sheikh, Linda Ehrl, Yorick Carroux, Laura Ximena Villanueva Guerra and Robert Stranz, the Davis Family, Lindsay Miller, Sascha Rimkus, Mats Green, Celia Solf, Mirja and Jeremy Silvermann, Britt and Walter Baugh, Inga Ericsson Fogh, Tedde and Lisbeth Åhlund, Pia Lambert, Johanna Paues Darlington, Alexander Sommerick, Chrischa Oswald, Bernadette Timmer-Nickel, David Noel, Francine Grünewald and Laurent Chauvat, Gisela and Edgar Matt, Eric Wahlforss, Ellen Weib, Julia Bentele, Mary Sherpe, Kurt Miller, Antje Taiga Jandrig, Anders More, Magnus Hedin, Sandra Johansson, Anders Jacobsson, Robin van der Kaa, the Büchel Family, Bianca Stella Deangelis, Zarifa Mohamad, Alanna Hale, Anne-Sophie Noel and Priska Tijdof, Oliver Zingg, Olaf Deharde, Hendrick Haase, Nina Trentmann, Antje Wever, Vilislava Petrova, Gerard Wilson, Katherine Sacks, Anna Winger, Timo Gässner, Markus Klosseck, Antonio Elena, and my friends around the world who have followed and supported me along the way. Without your good spirits there is nothing.